Skills in
Transactional Analysis
Counselling &
Psychotherapy

Series editor: Francesca Inskipp

Skills in Counselling & Psychotherapy is a new series of practical guides for trainees and practitioners. Each book takes one of the main approaches to therapeutic work and describes the core skills and techniques used within that approach.

Topics covered include

♦ how to establish and develop the therapeutic relationship
♦ how to help the client change
♦ how to assess the suitability of the approach for the client.

This is the first series of books to look at skills specific to the different theoretical approaches, making it ideal for use on a range of courses which prepare the trainees to work directly with clients.

Books in the series:

Skills in Gestalt Counselling & Psychotherapy
Phil Joyce & Charlotte Sills

Skills in Person-Centred Counselling & Psychotherapy
Janet Tolan

Skills in Cognitive Behaviour Counselling & Psychotherapy
Frank Wills

Skills in

Transactional Analysis Counselling & Psychotherapy

Christine **Lister-Ford**

Los Angeles | London | New Delhi
Singapore | Washington DC

First published 2002

Reprinted 2013

SAGE Publications Ltd
1 Oliver's Yard
55 City Road
London EC2A 4PU

SAGE Publications Inc.
2455 Teller Road
Thousand Oaks, California 91320

SAGE Publications India Pvt Ltd
B1/1 Mohan Cooperative Industrial Area
Mathura Road, New Delhi
New Delhi 110 044

SAGE Publications Asia-Pacific Pte Ltd
3 Church Street
#10-04 Samsung Hub
Singapore 049483

British Library Cataloguing in Publication data

A catalogue record for this book is available from the British Library

ISBN 978 0 7619 5696 4
ISBN 978 0 7619 5697 2 (pbk)

Library of Congress Control Number: 2001135937

Typeset by M Rules
Printed in Great Britain by Ashford Colour Press Ltd., Gosport, Hampshire.

For my dearest Jennie, who first introduced me to TA over 23 years ago and, without whom, neither I nor this book would have made it through the storm. Your innovative ideas, meticulous editing and inspirational suggestions have transformed the quality and lucidity of the text. Thank you for so generously giving your time, care and knowledge.

Contents

Acknowledgements

Every effort has been made to trace all the copyright holders, but if any have been inadvertantly overlooked the publishers will be pleased to make the necessary arrangement at the first opportunity.

Preface

Eric Berne was an inspired and creative theorist and practitioner who evolved practical and sophisticated ways of working with emotional problems. His classical principles and therapeutic techniques remain as useful today as they were when he first conceived them.

In this book, I draw on classical Bernian principles and approaches to demonstrate the art of TA practice. This is reflected in the notes and further reading. I have framed these principles within a contemporary relational approach to the therapeutic encounter, discussing what both the client and the counsellor are likely to experience.

I have written this book for students of counselling as well as for practitioners wanting to understand more about the practical application of TA theory. To get the best from this approach requires the reader to use the exercises throughout the text and to relate the ideas to client work as well as to themselves.

This is a book about process and practice. The text follows the typical pattern of working with a client using TA and allows for short-term and longer-term options. Concepts and skills are introduced at the stage of work when they are required so that the reader can build their skills base in tandem with the development of the counselling itself. Relevant in-depth theory can be followed up through the recommended reading.

Chapter 1 provides a background to the origins, philosophy, key assumptions and goals of TA counselling as well as its development and its application. An outline of the stages of the therapeutic process is given together with the basic therapeutic interventions in TA.

Part One focuses on the development of the counselling relationship – how to build the therapeutic alliance and create structures in which the counselling can begin.

Part Two demonstrates how the TA counsellor builds and deepens the client's awareness, resulting in the strengthening of their capacity to think clearly and solve problems. This generally leads to a reduction in the symptoms that were presented at the start.

Part Three guides the counsellor in deepening the work with the client, helping them to discover the history behind the problems through making contact with their inner child.

Part Four demonstrates how the counsellor enables the client to move toward personal autonomy through integrating and synthesizing the work. Finally, the ending of the counselling relationship is explored.

Apart from Chapter 1, each chapter provides exercises to help the counsellor incorporate the learning from each section. Aims and outcomes are clearly set out, together with the skills for each stage of the work.

In almost 20 years as a trainer and supervisor I have found that one of the best ways of learning for my students has been through the use of audiotapes of counselling sessions. I encourage students to tape their work with clients and make verbatim transcriptions of short segments of the work. This form of self-reflection is a great way to self-supervise. You will find that you gain more from this book if you use tapes of sessions as an aid to the exercises that are given throughout the text. This will help you to see how you are using the theories and skills presented. Remember when using this form of recording to do so in an ethical way and to erase the tapes after use.

My thanks to Francesca Inskipp, the series editor, for giving me the opportunity to write this book and allowing me the freedom to develop the book in my own way, and for being steadfast in her encouragement and support; and to Alison Poyner of Sage who has been available, flexible and responsive as the book neared completion.

I am grateful to my clients, students and supervisees who have taught me so much – I hope what I have tried to convey does justice to their wisdom and skilled teaching; to my many teachers of TA throughout the world who have inspired me to learn and deepened my understanding; and finally to Becky my trainer, Amru my tennis coach and Tessie and Bethy my two Scotties, who have all kept me active during long months of writing!

I hope you too enjoy your journey with TA.

Outline of the Five Stages of TA Counselling

In the first stage, the client *tells their story* as the counsellor guides them through focused listening, comments and questions that enable important information to surface. During this phase the *therapeutic alliance* develops and when the client is ready a contract for the counselling is agreed.

In the second stage, the client develops *insight and awareness* and they begin to know and understand the nature and origins of their problems. Symptoms begin to abate and the client generally begins to feel more in charge. As this happens emotions will begin to surface.

The third stage, *working through*, includes the *emergence of buried emotions and associated memories*. The client releases held emotions related to going against their human wants and needs and this usually involves some grieving for their lost opportunities. This stage often provokes feelings of anxiety as the client re-evaluates their life; it is often the most challenging phase for both counsellor and client.

When the client has expressed these feelings and let go of past hurt they feel freer and clearer about themselves and their life. They move on to the fourth stage, *redecision*. The client begins to let go of script roles, making choices and decisions about how they want to live and be. They will experiment with being different both inside and outside the counselling setting. The counsellor's main role is to provide positive support to the client. The counselling contract is coming to completion.

Finally, in the fifth stage, *succeeding and ending counselling*, the client achieves their goals, and they review the work and make an ending.

1 · What Is Transactional Analysis?

Transactional Analysis, because of its clear-cut statements rooted in easily accessible material, because of its operational natures, and because of the small size of its specialized vocabulary (consisting in practice of only five words: Parent, Adult, Child, game, and script), offers an easily learned framework.

Eric Berne, *Principles of Group Treatment*

You will find TA a lively, dynamic and intelligent way to work, allowing for creativity and the use of intuition. TA practitioners have a wide array of concepts from which to draw understanding for situations ranging from the simple to the more complex.

TA has its roots in psychoanalysis, draws from the cognitive and behaviourist schools, is informed by existential thought, employs phenomenological method and has the client at the centre. As TA continues to develop its theory, skills and relational mode it seeks to integrate and adapt the most useful from other approaches into practice.

TA integrates the cognitive, emotional, behavioural and physical in both its psychological concepts and its application. Many would include a spiritual dimension, too. TA has a theory of mind, a theory of emotion, a theory of behaviour, and a theory of the links between these areas and the somatic or bodily experience. This makes it a uniquely comprehensive and adaptable approach for counselling and psychotherapy, allowing flexible and highly focused formulations of client needs and targeted interventions.

Origins and influences

Eric Berne, an American psychiatrist, first formulated and developed TA ideas, concepts and skills. At the start of the 1940s Berne began psychoanalytic training with the intention of eventually practising himself. During the course of his training Berne met two people who were to prove particularly influential in the development of his ideas. This led to his movement away from traditional psychoanalysis toward the development of a radical and creative reformulation of psychotherapeutic concepts, language and practice. Paul Federn catalysed Berne's interest in *ego psychology* and helped him develop his thinking about the structure of the personality. The ego state model of the person with its three aspects, Parent, Adult and Child, which Berne eventually evolved, is now the most well-known cornerstone of TA theory and practice.

Erik Erikson, another key influence, brought out in Berne an abiding aware-ness of the importance of *social and developmental influences* on the formation of personality. Many key concepts in TA have a developmental perspective, recog-nizing that early experiences mould and eventually form internal psychological structures that determine our actions.

Berne developed his ideas in several ways, through his therapeutic practice, through his writing and in discussion with colleagues. An avid learner, he used every opportunity to deepen his knowledge and experience. What followed was a rapid development in the dissemination of TA owing to its easy accessibility and creative approach. Berne was surprised when his books, originally intended as readable clinical texts for psychoanalysts, became best sellers and sold millions throughout the world. TA was taken up and used as a tool in many different areas. Berne's work has played a significant part in changing mental health practice over the last 50 years and today most counselling courses introduce students to basic TA theory.

Basic building blocks of TA

The basic building blocks that will be used throughout this book are the corner-stones of TA theory and practice. They involve the analysis of ego states, transactions, games and script.

Model of the person: the ego state model

The ego state model itself is a developmental one, charting significant early expe-riences (Child), the important influences of others (Parent) and the integration of these into a here-and-now working reality (Adult). Significant failures to meet a child's needs eventually lead to psychological weakening and significant intrapsy-chic flaws. Ego states and life script map the internal and interpersonal difficulties that can arise when early needs go unmet.

Theory of communication: transactions

Another unique aspect of TA is its theory of communication, transactional analy-sis proper, which allows understanding both of how the internal world influences interactions with others and the patterns of these interactions themselves. This gives us options and choices for improving communication and is valuable in the therapeutic relationship.

Psychological games

Games are repetitive patterns of behaviour that lead to a familiar 'bad' feeling. Although we are usually aware of these patterns to some extent, we are not aware of the psychological drives and 'unfinished business' that underpin them. Games reinforce and maintain the individual's script.

Script

Script is an unconscious life plan made in early childhood and based on decisions made in response to external influence and internal vulnerability.

Through the analysis of these four aspects of individual personality the client's consciousness is raised and he becomes empowered to take control of his life and change his destiny.

Goals of TA counselling and psychotherapy

Autonomy

> Human potential is as infinite as human adaptability. Each generation of parents has the option to oppress its offspring with age-old curses, or to protect its children's spontaneity, encourage their awareness, and respond to their intimate needs that they may reach their full potential. Pushing through to the surface, people's basic nature is like a perennial virgin spring, ever ready to feed life with its sweet waters.[1]

Autonomy, developing our capacity for awareness, spontaneity and intimacy, is at the heart of TA philosophy and its practice. The major goal of TA therapeutic work is the progression toward autonomy and the recovery of its three capacities. Most of us encounter limits in one or more of these areas as life presents challenges with which we feel ill prepared to deal.

Awareness

Awareness is the ability to live in the present moment, perceiving it without interruption. Many of us, without being aware of this, avoid living in the moment for much of the time. We ruminate about the past and plan for the future, constantly thinking about what comes next. Vibrant and clear contact with the here-and-now experience and the stimulation of our senses is clouded and interrupted by memories of past influences, parental or cultural instructions of how to be in the world and how to perceive it.

Example

Mary, a newly bereaved, elderly widow, had enjoyed a traditional marriage where the sharing of tasks was in accordance with gender roles. Her husband had always managed their finances and during counselling it emerged that she believed she was unable to do this. She was feeling very anxious as a result of her difficulty. Awareness of her hidden abilities in this area was clouded by cultural and social norms that had led her to see managing finances as a man's job. Permitting herself a wider vision of her abilities was challenging and raised unwelcome questions about the way in which she had previously chosen to live. To take hold of her financial skills, Mary had to face the painful realization that she had always been capable in this area. What her husband had made look arduous and difficult she found easy. Mary battled with feelings of guilt, anger and disloyalty before she was able to come to terms with owning her acumen.

Spontaneity

Spontaneity is the ability to put aside familiar, well-exercised options, and choose according to what seems to fit the moment. The unpredictability inherent in being spontaneous is part of the risk, the gamble with the unknown, and is, of course, one of the main reasons why truly being spontaneous often evokes anxiety from which it is tempting to shy away by choosing familiar options. Learning to say yes to what we want and no to what we don't want sounds simple, yet as we all know it carries the risk of disapproval or rejection.

Intimacy

Intimacy involves exposing our vulnerability to others: showing how we really think, feel and behave without the need to mask ourselves in what we imagine the other person wants or can cope with; being prepared to meet the other person and to listen to them unimpeded by our own wants, needs or projections. Intimacy is high-risk stuff, only possible with a limited number of people and only for some of the time. To engage in intimacy requires us to take off the masks we wear and be less predictable. This gives us the opportunity for a rich and meaningful experience – to be valued for who we really are and for what we really think and feel, finding a sense of worth through the love and understanding of another. But there are no guarantees and we may find ourselves rejected or embarrassed in the process of taking the risk. The stakes are high. We might question if Mary would have taken these risks had her husband been alive.

Promoting autonomy and helping people recover lost aspects of their autonomy are delicate and sensitive matters. 'Autonomy', 'awareness', 'spontaneity' and 'intimacy' sound highly desirable. But the actual reality of reaching for them can be very challenging. TA counsellors must be careful to check what the client really wants to explore and whether, during that exploration, they might go into deeper waters than they had anticipated. Different people can tolerate different levels of discomfort. Many clients are prepared for this before they enter counselling and for others this comes as a surprise. The therapeutic journey needs to be carefully planned in order to prevent wounding, depression or psychological fragmentation.

Take a few moments to think about where you are in your life right now with these qualities/abilities:

◆ Which are most challenging for you?

◆ Identify those that it might be useful for you to strengthen.

Key Skills

A useful strategy is to give a 'mental health warning', explaining to the client that TA counselling, with its focus on heightening awareness, 'can change your life'. This statement is then explored with the client in detail in the first session in order to ascertain the desired level and goals of the counselling work.

Whilst espousing autonomy as a value it is absolutely crucial not to thrust our own vision of it onto the client. Freedom of choice includes the right to say 'no', and respecting this is a *prima facie* duty of the counsellor.

> Intimacy, awareness and spontaneity are innately human and, even if crushed, will re-emerge again and again within each succeeding generation.[2]

Philosophical base: a humanistic psychology

Although having strong roots in psychoanalytic theory, TA is a humanistic psychology. Part of Berne's early motivation was to evolve an approach to working with people that was not shrouded in mystique and which allowed for mutuality of relationship by recognizing that equally important contributions are made by counsellor and client alike. Ownership of the therapy belongs to the client. Berne wanted the language of TA to be easily understood by the client as well as the therapist. He saw the creation of a shared language as a real means of creating equality. As part of achieving this end, Berne took common American terms and phrases and turned them into technical therapeutic language: 'games', 'script', 'strokes', 'rackets', 'I'm OK, you're OK' are some of the better-known examples.

TA counselling emphasizes a number of fundamental humanistic principles, as follows.

Respect for all

Prime amongst TA's humanistic principles is respect for self and other, 'I'm OK, you're OK', expressed in the content and through the process of TA practice. This idea sounds deceptively straightforward. In fact, it is complex and sophisticated, often requiring subtle yet profound shifts in attitude. It is easy to believe in our own self-worth until circumstances challenge those things on which self-worth is based. Believing in the innate goodness, decency, and right to be respected of others is easy when we feel they deserve help and a better deal in life. It becomes more problematic when the material they bring touches on a personal sore spot or a passionately held moral principle, for example when the client holds values powerfully at odds with those of the counsellor. Each of us is susceptible in different ways, yet we all have our trigger points. 'I'm OK, you're OK' is a gritty and challenging philosophical position from which to practise. Inevitably most of us fail significantly from time to time. At such moments, avoiding self-judgement in favour of an honest appraisal of our shortcomings and the reasons for them can prove a rich source of self-supervision and learning.

Example

During the next few days notice when you feel OK and what situations, people and conversations take you up or down.

Personal responsibility

This is another key principle of TA. Self-agency is the key to responsibility. Just as the infant has to learn the complicated mechanics of how to control its limbs so that they move fluidly and allow coordinated movement so, emotionally, people need to learn the skilled coordination of their feelings, thoughts and behaviour. This means understanding how we process, control and manipulate ourselves; how we create the cause and effect of our experience. Personal responsibility is often misunderstood. Many think it wildly improbable and cite the many circumstances in which we do not control our destinies. Such a response fails to understand that we are describing the search for an inner state of being, not an external set of circumstances.

Taking responsibility for ourselves is a big undertaking. For most people it probably requires a lifetime's trial and error. It requires facing all manner of existential dilemmas – loneliness, guilt, fear and despair. Perhaps, ultimately, it is discovering peace of mind founded on experiencing the randomness of life's joys and pains and emerging intact with a keen sense of self, feeling satisfied to be who we are.

Example

In overcoming her anxiety and taking control of her life Mary chose to face the painful realization that she had lived her life from a position of dependency without achieving her potential. Coming as it did in the last season of her life both released her and led to reflections on what could have been.

Self-responsibility is the exercising of power – the power of choice. The choice is to accept that whilst neither external circumstances nor other people can be controlled, we can change our own inner experience. We do not have to feel according to the old ways. We do not have to respond like those we have taken as role models. We can choose responses that are genuine and fit our current lifestyle and who we are today.

Mythology, literature and religion contain many examples of this difficult journey. A moving example of self-determination is provided by Viktor Frankl.[3] Despite the horrors of incarceration he found ways to experience meaning and purpose whilst living in a German concentration camp. He discovered that when we are able to choose our inner experience we are truly free, because we are in charge of our own destiny, no matter how dire our outer circumstances. This is the aim which is at the centre of TA philosophy and practice.

Example

Think back to a time when you have made choices and decisions to take responsibility for your life. What did you have to give up to make these choices?

Change is possible

Except in instances of organic damage, it is usually possible to bring about therapeutic change providing:

◆ The client is motivated.

◆ The practitioner is using the right approach.

◆ The goals are realistic.

◆ The environment offers enough support.

Theory of change

Berne believed that human beings have:

> A built-in drive to health, mental as well as physical . . . mental development and emotional development has been obstructed . . . the therapist has only to remove the obstructions for the patient to grow naturally in his own direction . . . The therapist's task, therefore, is to locate the healthy areas in each patient's personality so as to nurture them and strengthen their potential.[4]

Berne shared the belief of other humanistic therapists that human beings strive toward health and will, if given the right conditions, flourish and grow.

Berne encouraged therapists to strive for what he called 'cure' or transformation: the unquenchable ability of people to rise above circumstances, past history and self-destructive inner drives and impulses. This gives TA its defining humanistic qualities. The vision is of a person able to set herself free from even the most constricting of psychological and social bonds, to reclaim the spirit within. To work with these values is a challenge for the counsellor. It means that we must engage in our own 'cure' and offer a high standard of professional service to our clients.

Cure means that we are no longer driven to replay the past through psychological game playing or by following the script messages. Instead we are free to live in the moment, risking intimacy, learning from mistakes and fulfilling our potential. We let go of held pain, grieve for our losses, forgive those who have failed us, leaving behind whatever baggage we have been carrying. We remember our past but do not repeat it. This is an ongoing journey which we all need to address for ourselves as we work with clients.

The beautiful thing about script cure is that it releases the next generation from the burdens of the past. Individuals who have transformed themselves in this way do not pass on to their own children destructive and limiting script messages.

TA in practice

Social psychiatry

Social psychiatry, as it was first known, and which today we might call social awareness and positive anti-discrimination, has always been to the forefront of TA thinking and practice. Originally one of the goals of TA was to act as an agent for social change. Treating all people equally and making TA available to as many as possible have always been at the heart of TA practice. Toward this end transactional analysts have developed creative ways of using TA. Over the last 30 years the application of TA within different fields has been shaped and formalized and it is now possible to train and qualify as a transactional analyst in four different fields: psychotherapy, education, organizational and counselling.

TA psychotherapy

Clearly Berne's original intention was the application of TA to clinical work or psychotherapy. He developed a methodology and a language that were outside the domain of medical psychiatry. His aim was to make them accessible to professionals in related fields, to lay people and in particular to the patients themselves. His goal was 'script' cure which he originally called *psychoanalytic cure.*

TA in education

TA in education is a unique application of therapeutic concepts, taking a directly educative and preventive role with children, parents and educators. TA principles are used as a means of teaching emotional literacy and empowering children to became emotionally and interpersonally skilled.

TA in organizations

TA in organizations applies TA principles to organizational contexts in teaching effective communication and solving systemic problems. Many companies employ TA consultants to help them create effective working environments for their staff, reduce stress and maximize creativity.

TA counselling

TA counselling is the most recent field to be developed. Counsellors working within a wide range of social contexts utilize TA to make their work more effective. In 1995 the Counselling Subcommittee of the International Transactional Analysis Association (ITAA) and the European Association for Transactional Analysis (EATA) defined TA counselling:

Transactional Analysis Counselling is a professional activity within a contractual relationship. The counselling process enables clients or client systems to develop awareness, options and skills for problem management and personal development in daily life through the enhancement of their strengths and resources. Its aim is to increase autonomy in relation to their social, professional and cultural environment.

TA is used in a variety of therapeutic approaches including individual, group, couples and family work. TA can be used in short-term focused counselling, medium-term work, and long-term counselling and in-depth psychotherapy.

Professional responsibility

Berne wrote and spoke passionately about professional responsibility. His notion of 'cure' was a metaphor to remind the therapist that they are in that role solely to help the client get better. He urged us to become 'real doctors' in the sense that we help the person heal and don't waste time intellectualizing or engaging in meaningless chat with our clients.

Respect for the client is paramount and a TA therapist should demonstrate this to her clients in her manner and behaviour. For example, we make sure that we are thoughtful, kind, ethical and prompt in meeting the client at the designated time. Many clients have had negative experiences with health professionals: this is a significant discount and immediately sets up a situation of being one-down.

Berne wrote that:

1 A 'real doctor' is specifically oriented throughout his training toward curing his patients, and that is his overriding consideration throughout his practice.
2 A 'real doctor' can plan his treatment so that at each phase he knows what he is doing and why he is doing it.
3 A 'real doctor' clearly distinguishes research and experimentation from good medical or surgical care and the former is always subsidiary to the latter.
4 A 'real doctor' takes sole and complete responsibility for the welfare of his patients.[5]

Open communication

Berne insisted on open communication, which was a radical move in psychiatry at that time. It means that whatever we have to say about the therapy needs to be said directly to the client. The therapist does not hold professional secrets or talk in a derogatory way about her clients. She shares the information that both parties need to know, such as:

- whether or not the therapist can help the client
- the goals of the therapy
- the stages of the therapy and what is likely to happen
- how long the therapy will take
- problems that might occur because of the changes made through therapy
- information regarding the therapy
- the professional status of the therapist.

This way of relating is what distinguishes a TA practitioner in her behaviour with both clients and colleagues.

TA as a worldwide approach

What many people involved in TA particularly appreciate is that it is an approach popular throughout the world. TA seems to be acceptable to the majority of cultures, social groups and religions and is therefore a useful tool for transcultural work.

In most countries it is possible to find a TA practitioner, an official training programme and local study groups as well as a national TA organization. The ITAA hosts its annual conference around the world, the EATA organizes TA in Europe, and the Institute of Transactional Analysis (ITA) coordinates within the United Kingdom.

Process of TA therapy: the five stages

TA counselling has five main stages. It is useful to share this information with the client early in the counselling so that they have an understanding of the process and what they might experience along the way. The layout of the chapters follows these stages through.

1 The client *tells their story* as the counsellor guides them through focused listening, comments and questions that enable important information to surface. During this phase the *therapeutic alliance* develops and when the client is ready a contract for the counselling is agreed.

2 The client develops *insight and awareness* and they begin to know and understand the nature and origins of their problems. Symptoms begin to abate and the client generally begins to feel more in charge. As this happens emotions will begin to surface.

3 The *working through* stage includes the *emergence of buried emotions and associated memories*. The client releases held emotions related to going against their human wants and needs and this usually involves some grieving for their lost opportunities. This stage often provokes feelings of anxiety as the client re-evaluates their life; it is often the most challenging phase for both counsellor and client. When the client has expressed these feelings and let go of past hurt they feel freer and clearer about themselves and their life, and they move on to the next stage.

4 The *redecision* stage. The client begins to let go of script roles, making choices and decisions about how they want to live and be. They will experiment with being different both inside and outside the counselling setting. The counsellor's main role is to provide positive support to the client. The counselling contract is coming to completion.

5 *Succeeding and ending counselling.* Finally, when the client has achieved their goals they review the work and make an ending.

What are the distinguishing features of the TA practitioner?

So what qualities does the TA counsellor need to develop to distinguish herself as an authentic practitioner of TA? An in-depth training is essential; however, TA trainees need to engage in a personal journey in order to become aware of their own script. Only in this way can they become effective and authentic practitioners of TA.

The following list gives an indication of the values and goals involved in the personal development of the TA practitioner:

◆ the pursuit of autonomy in self and others

◆ respect for self and others – 'I'm OK, you're OK'

◆ personal responsibility and self-knowledge

◆ a humanistic stance

◆ open communication: includes the client in discussion of the therapy, does not hold secret knowledge of the client or talk about them without their express permission, is truthful

◆ avoids psychological games

◆ cooperative

◆ emotionally literate

◆ makes clear contracts

◆ abides by the TA codes of ethics and practice of their national TA organization.

This is not to say that TA counsellors are perfect; no one achieves all of these things all of the time. We are all human and live in a world that continually pressurizes us to be somebody else. However, the client should at least expect the TA counsellor to practise, as far as possible, what they preach.

Berne comments with some humour:

> Psychotherapists are parapeople, but they are entitled to laugh occasionally just like real people – only for a few seconds, however, then they must get back to work.[6]

In the following chapters we will explore the application of the TA model, the process of the work and the application of TA skills in counselling and psychotherapy practice.

Notes

1   C. Steiner, *Scripts People Live* (Bantam, New York, 1974), p. 384.
2   Ibid., p. 384.
3   V. Frankl, *Man's Search for Meaning* (Hodder & Stoughton, London, 1962).
4   E. Berne, *Principles of Group Treatment* (Grove, New York, 1966), p. 63.
5   Ibid., p. xvii.
6   Ibid., p. 338.

Further reading on TA theory

Berne, E. (1961) *Transactional Analysis in Psychotherapy*. New York: Grove.
Steiner, C. (1974) *Scripts People Live*. New York: Grove.
Stewart, I. (1992) *Eric Berne*. London: Sage.
Stewart, I. and Joines, V. (1987) *TA Today*. Nottingham: Lifespace.
Tilney, T. (1998) *Dictionary of Transactional Analysis*. London: Whurr.

Part One

The Counselling Relationship

2 · Beginning the Relationship

The first meeting between client and counsellor is a momentous occasion. As with any new relationship the atmosphere is charged with hopes, expectations, fears and anxieties. For the client the stakes are high. They have admitted, first to themselves, and now to you, that all is not well. This immediately places them in a vulnerable position. They have exposed a tender place in themselves. In itself, this is an act of considerable courage. This admission carries with it an implicit statement of the client's felt powerlessness – that on their own they are finding it difficult to solve a problem and they want your help. For the client the big question is, 'Can my problem be solved?'

Your main goals are to:

◆ meet the client

◆ find out about the client's difficulty

◆ help the client to find out about the way you work and what you can offer

◆ answer the client's questions.

The most important outcomes from this first meeting are:

◆ to allow the client to make an informed initial assessment about whether you and TA counselling are what they want

◆ to decide whether or not you can offer the client what they want

◆ to decide whether or not the two of you will make an initial counselling contract

◆ when counselling is to go ahead, to agree a provisional approach.

Meeting the client

Creating the right emotional environment

In requesting your help the client is telling you that he believes you have the ability to make a difference to his circumstances through your knowledge and therapeutic skills. The client is taking a leap of faith, placing his belief in you and your ability to help. It is a hard-bitten counsellor who does not feel awe and humility in the face of such an act of trust by another human being.

Rapport

Creating the right emotional environment into which to welcome a fellow human on such a quest is obviously important. Establishing rapport is the first step. The counsellor will offer a relaxed, welcoming and accepting setting in which the client can begin to feel suspension of any unwelcome judgements (either yours or theirs) and an invitation to explore their problems. Rapport is shown both non-verbally and verbally. It begins by paying attention to the client's basic needs for physical well-being, for example:

◆ pre-counselling information – such as how to get to the venue and information about parking

◆ a warm physical environment

◆ clarifying the location of the toilet

◆ smoking facilities

◆ the offer of a drink

◆ clear information about whether there is a waiting area

◆ checking if seating is adequate and comfortable.

Equally important is the setting and maintenance of time boundaries:

◆ starting and finishing on time

◆ specifying the length of the session

◆ the initial time frame of how many sessions to expect

◆ letting the client know when the session is coming to a close.

Being attentive to such matters shows respect for the client and gives an immediate, implicit message that you are a counsellor who will take charge of the boundaries in an appropriate and thoughtful manner.

Empathy

Empathy is the second quality needed to create a welcoming atmosphere. Empathy is the ability to tune into another person, to have a felt sense of their experience without losing one's own experience of reality. It is coming as close to another human being as it is possible to do without merging or joining with them and becoming part of them. Some writers suggest we are born with an innate capacity for empathic attunement.[1] Many of us have learned to hold back our empathic connection, seeing only what we are supposed to 'see' and screening out the rest. Smell, taste, touch, hearing and 'gut' feelings tend to be 'tamed' in the same way. The TA counsellor needs to learn to retune their senses. They will then have a rich source of valuable information that when used will deepen empathic contact. Careful observation of the client, together with a delicate attunement to what they are trying to convey through verbal and non-verbal signalling, are the basis for the development of empathy.

Example
Jane noticed her new client smelled strongly of cigarettes. His stomach was rumbling and his manner tense. He had dark circles under his eyes. As she cross-matched this information against her own internal response to him she noticed she was feeling tense and slightly anxious. This became a rich source of knowledge, which Jane used to begin to speak with the client about his life and feeling state.

Exercise
Developing empathy: the fortune teller
With a partner, take turns to be the 'fortune teller' with the other in the client role.

1 Notice what you observe using your senses.
- Shake their hand. What do you feel through their handshake?
- What can you see in their skin tone, face, nails, hands and clothing?
- What can you smell? This might take a minute or two of going inward and being still to reflect on a person's odour. Unless it is very apparent, we often screen this out. Perfume conveys a message and should be taken into account.
- What can you hear? Body noises, breathing, voice tone?
- What is your 'gut' feeling as you take in the other person? What do you experience inside?
- Imagine yourself in their clothes. How do you imagine their clothing feels against their skin?

◆ Imagine any taste they may have in their mouth. What taste is foreground in your mouth as you sit with this person?

2 Describe to your partner what you imagine about their current lifestyle
using only the 'information' gained in this exercise.

3 Share what you experienced in taking these risks.

Having used this exercise over many years, I find that my trainee counsellors
are amazed at the depth of information they 'pick up'. They go on to develop
a greater confidence in their own intuitive skills through the use of finely
tuned perception.

Complementary transactions

Rapport and empathy are best conveyed through complementary transactions,
that is, talking the same language as the client by ensuring that initially we
acknowledge their frame of reference by responding to their cues. This is done by
responding to the client from the ego state (or part of us) which they address. The
functional ego state model provides a map for understanding how people com-
municate. It helps us to identify which ego state is prominent in personal
interactions, giving the counsellor information as to which ego state to address
first. Each ego state functions in a distinctive way.

The model is shown in Figure 2.1. The three domains are as follows:

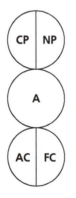

Figure 2.1 Functional ego state model

Reprinted with permission from Tony Tilney. *Dictionary of Transactional Analysis*. London: Whurr Publishers.

◆ *Parent* The Parent operates through values, opinions and judgements and functions in two distinct modes. The *Nurturing Parent* (NP) offers nurturing, support and care. The *Controlling Parent* (CP) provides safe boundaries and limits, with the intention to protect. These modes also have a negative function. The Nurturing Parent can be over-protective or smothering. The Controlling Parent can be over-controlling and critical.

◆ *Adult* The Adult (A) is the domain of rationality and reason. It functions to mediate between Parent and Child in order to evolve a view that takes account of both; it checks out and tabulates the external world and brings realism to bear on the internal view.

◆ *Child* The Child expresses itself through feelings and instinctive reactions; it seeks to meet its own needs. It functions in two distinct modes. The *natural* or *Free Child* (FC) responds in an immediate, socially unconstrained way. The *Adapted Child* (AC) responds on the basis of internalized social learning, and seeks to adapt to the imagined or real demands of other people.

Example

Mary felt overwhelmed by the loss of her husband and wanted a sympathetic and nurturing response. An exchange is illustrated in Figure 2.2. Mary is in Adapted Child; she addresses (S1) her counsellor's Nurturing Parent, and she receives a nurturing response (R1) back.

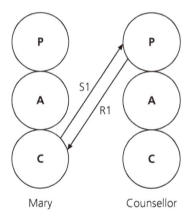

Figure 2.2 Mary's exchange

Mary (S1): I'm not sure where to start, it's all a bit overwhelming. (AC)
Counsellor (R1): Start wherever feels right, it will take some time for you to say all you want to. (NP)

Case example: Tom

Tom arrived 20 minutes early for his appointment; he apologized repeatedly for the inconvenience and gave the impression of feeling embarrassed. He was well dressed in an almost creaseless dark suit, sparkling white shirt, muted tie and gleaming black shoes. After the briefest hesitation he offered to go away again and return at the appointed time.

His counsellor greeted him warmly (rapport), assured him that people sometimes arrive early for important appointments (empathy), offered him some tea and showed him where he could wait (rapport). Tom's facial muscles visibly relaxed.

Transactionally, at the verbal level, the exchange is as follows:

Tom (S1): I'm sorry to be early, is it inconvenient?
Counsellor (R1): I'm glad to see you! People are often early for important appointments.

This exchange is a complementary Adult–Adult one, as shown in Figure 2.3.

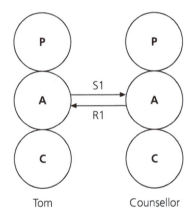

Figure 2.3 Tom's exchange at the verbal level

Reprinted with permission from Souvenir Press Ltd. Eric Berne (1961) *Transactional Analysis in Psychotherapy*. London: Souvenir Press.

At the non-verbal level, Tom is saying quite a lot more:

Tom (S2): This meeting really matters to me and I want to get it right. Am I acceptable?
Counsellor (R2): I can see your commitment and your nervousness. You are welcome here.

Because these messages are expressed non-verbally, the music behind the words, they are called *ulterior transactions* and are diagrammed as in Figure 2.4.

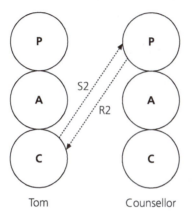

Tom   Counsellor

Figure 2.4 Tom's exchange at the non-verbal level

Reprinted with permission from Souvenir Press Ltd. Eric Berne (1961) *Transactional Analysis in Psychotherapy.* London: Souvenir Press.

Rapport and empathy are both communicated at the verbal and the non-verbal or ulterior level. Rapport is a proactive process, here created by a warm welcome through providing a pleasant environment into which the client feels truly invited. Empathy is a responsive process and depends upon an accurate reading and decoding of the client's internal world:

◆ their feelings about commencing counselling (Child ego state)
◆ their values and judgements about it (Parent ego state)
◆ their experience of the reality of it (Adult ego state).

The counsellor's understanding of the client is then reflected back with some important additions:

◆ acceptance of the client's reality as valid and true
◆ offering an additional piece of emphasis, the counsellor's own *presence*.

Presence

Presence is showing interest in tuning into another person in an active and appropriate way. It is letting the client know they are making an impact on you. Tom's counsellor stopped what she had been doing to spend time greeting him and showing him where to wait. True presence requires us to put aside our own needs and bring the client into the central focus of our attention. This may sound a simple thing to do, yet many counsellors find it takes practice. It requires the counsellors to deal with their own internal and external distractions and to silence these. To be present is to be still, calm and focused. Initiating a new relationship with a client is like any other new relationship, charged with uncertainty. We may be tense or anxious about ourselves, overly confident as a way of masking uncertainty, or using the professional role to hide our internal experiences. Developing presence takes time. Experience helps and self-awareness is the key.

> **Exercise**
> **Preparing to meet a new client**
> Before you meet a new client for the first time, take 10 minutes alone in a peaceful place to prepare yourself. You can set this up as a role play with a partner if you prefer.
>
> ◆ As you sit alone, notice what you feel inside about meeting this new person.
> ◆ Notice how you are feeling physically: do you need anything?
> ◆ What do you imagine the client will think of you?
> ◆ Does this remind you of anything?
> ◆ What images or associations come to mind?
> ◆ Check out what belongs in the past to other relationships.
> ◆ Tell yourself two positive things about the way you relate to new people.
> ◆ Take some deep breaths and go to meet the client.

Recognition of the client using positive strokes

To be present with another person also means giving overt recognition to them through positive feedback, called a *positive stroke*.

The counsellor needs to recognize the huge step the client has made. Strokes need to be carefully calibrated to match the client's nature: a shy client needs a low-key stroke, a more expressive client needs a more voluble one.

Example

[*voluble*] You've taken a really big step in coming today!

[*low key*] It's been nice to see you today.

Key skills

In the initial meeting with the client the following skills will enable you to establish potent contact that will make an impact on your client. This will help them to feel you are interested and involved from the outset. In themselves these skills will instil hope in the client that counselling might enable them to work through and understand their difficulties.

◆ Convey *professional authority.*
◆ Demonstrate *sensitivity* to the trust that the client is placing in you.
◆ Establish *rapport.*
◆ Develop *empathic attunement.*
◆ Establish *complementary transactions.*
◆ Demonstrate *presence.*
◆ Recognize the client with *positive strokes.*

Talking the client's language

Let the client say 'hello' in his or her own way. Two things are important to notice: the first transaction and the first few minutes. The *first transaction* the client makes will usually be one of the purest expressions of who, currently, they are and what, currently, they are experiencing.

During the first few minutes focus on the client and ask yourself the following questions:

◆ How are they entering the relationship with me?

◆ How do they present themselves?

◆ How do they use their energy?

◆ Which ego state is dominant (a) in the client (b) in the counsellor?

◆ What kind of self-protective strategies do they use to keep painful matters or awareness at bay?

◆ How do they view you and your role?

Example

[*clipped*] Good morning! Rodney Peterson, Sales Manager, Compton Engineering. I have
  an appointment with Mrs James at 10.00 o'clock on a confidential matter.

[*tearful*] Thank you for seeing me so quickly; I don't know what I'd have done otherwise.
  I'm in a terrible state.

[*smiling*] Hi, I'm Lucy, our mutual friend George suggested I contact you.

[*gasping*] I'm on a parking meter; I'm out of change. Have you got a pound coin?

First transactions are unique. No two are ever quite the same. They are an exciting moment when, for the first time, the client is revealed in person. Apart from
the words the client speaks, posture, gesture, facial expression, breathing, voice
tone, pitch and pace are important clues to the client's context. All are part of the
first transaction.

The first transaction starts the *first few minutes*. Berne spoke of the first three
minutes as key.[2] By highlighting such a brief time span he was drawing attention
to the need of the counsellor to be alert from the start because the whole of the
client's current reality, as well as their script, will be expressed in an encoded
form and, possibly, even the probable outcome of the counselling. The first three
minutes should not be defined in a rigid and uncompromising way, but simply
used to identify some key features of the client.

The first transaction and the first three minutes may take place on the telephone, on the walk to the counselling room or inside it. Managing this time so as
not to miss this vital contact is crucial.

Exercise
- Tape record the session with the client and transcribe the first three
  minutes.
- Listen to the client's voice tone, breathing and the words they use.
- Recall their non-verbal signals.
- Recall your own internal 'gut' response and notice your verbal and non-
  verbal responses.
- As far as you can, answer the questions listed earlier for the first transaction.

Case example: Angela

Angela began introducing herself to her counsellor with the comment, 'Well, I finally made it.' She seemed nervous and tense and looked tearful in those first few minutes. She described feeling 'sick in the pit of my stomach', anxiety and panic as she drove into work each day. As personal assistant to the chief executive of a large company, she carried a lot of responsibility. She felt 'on the brink of a nervous breakdown' and was afraid she would 'lose it' and cause chaos in the firm. On entering the office she battled to 'push down' her feelings but this left her 'drained, tense and irritable'. After struggling for several months, seeking counselling was her 'only hope'.

Important features in Angela's story
The counsellor recognized several important features in Angela's story.

1 *Observation*
   ◆ Whether or not she sought counselling help had been touch and go. (First trans-action.)
   ◆ In itself, arriving at the first session was a big achievement. (First transaction.)
   Action
   ◆ At some stage in the first meeting it would be important to stroke Angela for doing this. (First transaction → stroke.)

2 *Observation*
   ◆ Angela's feelings were strongly to the fore. (Non-verbal signs of tearfulness and dis-tress, including sad expression, a slight tremor in her voice as if she was not quite in control of it, a subtle rounding of her shoulders and closing of her upper body.)
   Action
   ◆ An important set of complementary transactions would be to provide reassurance from Nurturing Parent to Adapted Child.

3 *Observation*
   ◆ Disabling anxiety and panic. (This would need to be an immediate area of focus and intervention to help attain some symptom relief.)
   ◆ Lack of self-containment, seeming almost out of control. (Help her to regain con-trol through strengthening her Adult functioning and her taking charge of her Child.)
   Action
   ◆ The counsellor would need to be seen to be in control and to instil hope that some-one else can help and can make a difference. (Change is possible.)

Exploring the problem

◆ Her symptoms of panic and anxiety were related to the office. What is the problem there? Why is there a problem? (Develop Angela's awareness of the relationship between the office and the symptoms.)

◆ Is the presenting problem the real one, or is it serving as a screen for another problem? (Explore this as a second stage of developing awareness later in the counselling.)

◆ Counselling is the only hope: what happens if this doesn't work for Angela? (Ask Angela quite soon about this. What has she tried that hasn't worked? Why didn't other things work? Is there a pattern to how things fail? Could this pattern occur in the counselling? How?)

Initial counselling plan

◆ The counsellor was aware of experiencing pressure to do it right for someone feeling so fragile. (Need to avoid this pitfall; keep own panic and anxiety at bay; stay empathic but don't merge with client's experience.)

◆ The immediate goal is to help Angela feel more in control. (Check later if Angela wants this.)

◆ The outcome of the counselling will depend on the client's ability to stay in Adult and contain her feelings. (The extent to which this is possible is not yet clear; review after two to three sessions.)

Key skills

Management and containment of the counsellor's emotional responses

To help you do this:

◆ Take time out before the session to 'centre' yourself.

◆ Remember that some clients feel overwhelmed by their difficulties and are often extremely anxious about this first meeting with you.

◆ Remind yourself that you are in a position of authority; you have knowledge and skills that will help guide both you and the client through this first session.

◆ If you feel anxious during the session, focus on keeping your body still and calm, breathe rhythmically and use economy of speech. Remember, less is more.

Structuring the first session

Structure hunger,[3] the need for structure and containment, is an innate human need. At no time is it felt more strongly than when we are in a new situation where we are vulnerable. An explanation of the structure of the first session should be given to the client after the first few minutes; this helps to lessen anxiety and shares control. At this point it is important to establish if the counsellor and their service are the right one for the client before encouraging the client to proceed further with expression of their psychological need. This is an important *protection* for the client. *Explanation*, explaining what will happen and why it will happen, is a critical intervention at several points in the counselling process. But, perhaps, this is never more so than in the very beginning when clients are usually most lacking in information and knowledge, both about the process itself and about the person of the counsellor.

There are many ways of structuring the first session. One of the major dilemmas for counsellors at this time is the need to impart clear information about the service, whilst allowing the client adequate opportunity to talk about their difficulties. Dividing the first session into two separate parts does this most easily.

1 the business meeting, during which the business and administrative contracts are discussed

2 the therapeutic meeting, when the therapeutic contract is explored and some preliminary agreement is made.

Extending the length of the first session by an extra 30 minutes provides the necessary time to discuss the nature of the service on offer, and allows the client an opportunity to decide whether they want to proceed to the therapeutic time. It also allows the client to keep their inner, private world protected and to stay more easily in Adult whilst they think over the terms and conditions. An informed choice is then more likely. Naturally the client will need prior notice about how this first meeting will differ from any subsequent ones in the way it is structured. It is good practice not to make a charge for the time spent describing the service. The client has a right to know the details of the service without being charged a fee for this. This practice increases client choice and helps avoid difficulties such as the client revealing something that they later regret, or the counsellor being told something that they feel unable to hold in confidence. All parties are protected.

Helping the client contain strong emotion whilst negotiating the contract

Sometimes a client will be so distressed that they feel compelled to 'pour out' their emotions before an initial contract has been discussed. Whilst it is important to remain sensitive to the client's need to express how they are feeling, it is equally vital to establish the basic working agreements before proceeding with counselling interventions that might take the client deeper into their feelings. Bear in mind the following points:

◆ Information given prior to the session will aid the process of keeping clear the boundary between the business and administrative contract and the therapeutic contact and contract.

◆ Hold back direct counselling interventions until the first 'business' part of the session is completed and basic working agreements have been agreed.

◆ If you proceed with helping the client to tell their story before the boundaries of confidentiality have been agreed, you could find yourself in a difficult situation.

◆ Offer a non-alcoholic drink at the beginning of the first session. This often enables clients to manage and contain their feelings until the therapeutic time begins.

Example

Pauline broke down into deep sobs the moment she entered the counselling room. She had never met the counsellor before and had not received any information prior to this first meeting. The counsellor said that she could see Pauline was deeply distressed and asked what the problem was. Pauline, by now crying and shouting, said that she was drinking heavily to 'blot out the fact that my 12-year-old daughter is sleeping with my husband!'

Another counsellor handled a similar situation in a different way. The counsellor acknowledged the client's distress without asking what the problem was, and explained the need to give information and agree a contract before proceeding with addressing the client's problems. She then gave the client a drink of water to help them compose themselves before going through the business and administrative contracts.

Key skills

◆ Provide information regarding the timing and structure of the first session.
◆ Protection.
◆ Explanation.

- Keep to the structure of the session.
- Agree the basic working agreements before engaging in direct therapeutic interventions.

Describing the service and establishing an initial working agreement

In describing the service, the counsellor needs to explain both what the service is and how it works. Clear explanations are needed, and the client should be given plenty of opportunity to ask clarifying questions or for further information. At times *reassurance* may be needed to help ease worries which have no actual foundation but are reasonable concerns: for example, 'Will you tell the doctor everything I say?', 'Will my tutor have to know I've come for counselling?'

TA counsellors need to formulate a clear approach to this initial meeting. To hold back from giving full information because we fear the client may be put off is not good practice; equally, overloading the client with information is unhelpful. Some clients want to ask a lot of questions, whilst others want to know very little. Whilst tailoring what is said to suit client need, it is also essential to give an adequate outline of the service. Paying attention to our use of language is important. Unless a client specifically requests it, it is not a good idea to talk in technical terms; this has an alienating effect and serves to detract from good communication. Similarly, overuse of personal pronouns will invite the client into an emotional state at a vulnerable time and will inhibit their ability to listen to what is being said and appraise it. It is also likely to encourage a Parent–Child relationship and the beginnings of a strong emotional bond. On the whole, a friendly but neutral tone is probably most effective at this point; it will allow for Adult transactions and permit some emotional distance, so that if either the client or the counsellor does not wish to continue, this can be done without too much feeling of loss.

What to include in an initial explanation of TA

Include the following in an initial explanation.

The contract

- TA counselling is based on an explicitly agreed contract between counsellor and client.
- The contract will be reviewed periodically to check if it is being achieved and to reassess the way ahead.

◆ When the contract is not working, possible reasons for this will be looked at and, where necessary, a new contract made.

Equality of relationship

◆ The client and the counsellor are active and equal partners who bring different areas of knowledge and expertise.

◆ Both client and counsellor have the right to say 'yes' and 'no'.

◆ The counsellor is reliant on the client to say what is helpful and what is unhelpful, as well as anything that is causing concern.

Some normal reactions for the client which may give rise to concern

◆ Strong emotions, which may be painful, for example sadness or anger.

◆ Feeling worse before you feel better.

◆ The counselling isn't working.

Clear explanations convey to the client the philosophical base of TA by setting out what is on offer and involving them in the process.

Key skills

Explaining and contracting

◆ Keep explanations simple and free of jargon.
◆ Start with a free half-hour discussion of the business contract.
◆ Don't allow the client to tell her story until the limits of confidentiality are agreed.

Hidden expectations

In describing the counselling service we need to consider the context of the referral and the effect this might have on client expectations. For example, clients referred in medical settings where they are more usually described as patients may expect to continue in this role, anticipating that counselling is something that will be done to them. Sometimes people seek counselling in order to create documented evidence of personal distress in disputes with employers, insurance companies and marital partners. The counsellor needs to be aware of any hidden expectations and explore them directly with the client, considering how far (if at all) any such expectations will be met.

Limitations of counselling

The limits of the service, or what will *not* happen, need to be clearly described and discussed prior to commencing any therapeutic work in order to avoid undesirable outcomes arising from dashed hopes. Parents funding teenage children invariably nurse the hope that the child will come to more closely resemble their own view of a well-adapted young person. This rarely happens, and a disappointed parent may become an angry parent who withdraws funding on the basis that they are not receiving a good service. Sometimes clients fear particular outcomes: 'to change in ways my family won't like', 'that my marriage will break up'. No guarantees can be given. Where the client has such a strong prohibition it is often an indication that this may well be one of the areas where unwelcome change could occur. In such instances it is sometimes better not to start counselling than to risk an unwanted outcome. Counselling does not necessarily make people happier. Awareness can bring unwelcome realizations and cause discomfort; prospective clients need to know this.

Key skills

Hidden expectations and the limits of counselling

◆ Be aware of any hidden expectations and talk openly about them with the client.
◆ Be straight from the start about the limits of what you offer.
◆ It is better not to begin counselling than to risk an unwanted outcome.

Establishing an initial working agreement: the TA contract

Eric Berne defined a contract as an explicit 'bilateral commitment to a well defined course of action'.[4] He believed that for therapy to be effective, contracts need to be negotiated with all parties involved and need to include at least three aspects of the work:

◆ the business contract

◆ the administrative contract

◆ the therapeutic contract.

If necessary there will also be an organizational or three-way contract.

The business contract

The business contract describes the terms and conditions of the service on offer. The main counselling skill required is *explanation*: giving clear, simple explanations and actively ensuring the client has time to process, assimilate and clarify the information.

Time, length and frequency
Times of appointments, length, frequency and cost are the main elements to be covered in this area. TA counselling sessions are usually of 50 minutes duration, at weekly intervals, and at a mutually agreed time.

Fees
◆ Where an agency is providing the service, any fees are charged according to agency policy.

◆ Fees for independent practitioners are set according to the level of experience and qualification of the practitioner and in line with local going rates. The fee needs to have built into it the hidden costs of independent practice – the costs of running the service (room rental, refreshments, heating and so forth), administration time, the cost of supervision, accountancy costs, pension contributions, holiday time, and an 'unfit to work' factor that allows for times of normal ill-health that may occur in the working year.

◆ Current fees and procedures for making changes in fees should be clearly explained.

Policy and procedures for missed appointments
These need to be explained:

◆ Where an agency allows a time-limited number of sessions, does a missed appointment count towards the total number of sessions allowed?

◆ Where clients are fee paying, is there a charge for missed sessions?

◆ Is there an accepted cancellation period?

Out-of-hours contact
This should be clarified:

◆ Can you be reached out of hours? How is this done? When is it not possible?

- What happens if the client feels in need and you are unavailable?

- Are there fees for telephone contact?

Holiday periods

These should be described as relevant:

- For clients entering short-term counselling there may be no need to do this if their sessions will not coincide with a vacation period.

- For clients seeking long-term work the annual pattern of your holidays needs to be explained, describing when you will be unavailable and what alternative arrangements are possible should the client feel the need for counselling support.

Locum cover

It is good practice to provide locum cover for periods of absence for clients who might need this option of additional support:

- Working in tandem with a colleague and providing cover for each other is often a straightforward solution.

- Alternatively, making a specific one-way agreement with a colleague can also work well. Continuity of locum is advisable. You will come to understand each other's ways of working, and establish procedures for liaison.

- When a client needs to see a locum at different points in the counselling, it is easier if it is the same person; continuity enhances trust.

- An *ad hoc* approach to providing locum cover, whilst sometimes unavoidable, is the most stressful option for both client and counsellor.

Codes of ethics and practice

The codes of ethics and practice according to which the counsellor works should be identified.

Agency involvement

Any agency involvement should be explained including:

- Counsellor accountability to an agency or a referrer.

- The limits a third party may place on the context and nature of the service.

◆ Whether the total number of sessions may be extended at counsellor discretion or whether it is unchangeable.

◆ Whether reports of the work are required, and what is to be reported.

Increasingly many counsellors collate information about the business contract into a booklet to give to their clients. Clients can then read it at leisure and be assured they have all the relevant information without trying to memorize it.

The administrative contract

When the business contract has been agreed, the counsellor will move on to describe the administrative contract. This is the second phase of the preliminary half-hour meeting.

Confidentiality

One of the most important issues to discuss is confidentiality, and any limits placed on this. Generally, most TA counsellors would agree that where there are serious concerns about the safety either of the client, or of someone connected with them, confidentiality might be breached for the purposes of protection. Wherever feasible, every effort should be made to contact the client directly to discuss the proposed breach with the intention of keeping the client informed and discussing any action that could be taken conjointly by the counsellor and the client. Confidentiality is usually conditional upon clients not revealing illegal activity. Confidentiality does not extend to supervision, where all aspects of the work must be open for discussion for the purposes of learning and in the interests of safe practice. Client identity is generally protected. This is not always the case in the health services where, as a service provider, the agency has a duty to monitor the effectiveness of the treatment being received by each patient, and knowing the patient's identity can be an important aspect of this monitoring. Similar norms may apply to counsellors working in the legal system, for example with those convicted of a crime.

Establish informed consent by making sure that the client understands the limits of confidentiality. Nowadays many counsellors prefer to give this in writing to the client, adding the signatures of counsellor and client to the document.

Example of a two-way contract[5]

Marion Williams
Diploma in Therapeutic Counselling (Northern Guild for Psychotherapy)
22 Abbey Road, Woodbrough, WZ1 9AP
Tel.: 01515 425490

CONTRACT FOR COUNSELLING SERVICES

This is a contract between

Client

Practitioner

Confidentiality

All sessions will be conducted in confidence and may be recorded on audiotape. This confidence will be maintained, and applied to any and all records, in accordance with the Data Protection Act, except in the following instances:

1 Where the client gives consent for the confidence to be broken.
2 Where the counsellor is compelled by a court of law.
3 Where the information is of such gravity that confidentiality cannot be maintained; for example, where there is a possibility of harm to self or others and in cases of fraud or crime.
4 Where a locum has a need to know. This will normally be discussed with the client.
5 Where a referring GP or agency require a report. A copy of the report will be available to the client.

Sessions

The number of sessions will be . . . . subject to review and renegotiation.

Fees . . . . per session (reviewed on an annual basis).

1 *Cancellation of session by the clients*
A period of . . . . notice for individual sessions will be given, otherwise the session fee will be payable.
For group counselling sessions, fees are payable irrespective of attendance.

---

2 *Cancellation by the counsellor*
The client will be given reasonable notice wherever possible.

3 *Periods of absence*
A locum psychotherapist will be available on request.

4 *Termination of counselling*
. . . . sessions will be required as notice.

Code of ethics and practice

Marion Williams works in accordance with the Codes of Ethics and Practice of The Northern Guild for Psychotherapy.

Initial therapeutic contract

To explore probable sources of anxiety being experienced by the client and to conjointly develop strategies for managing these feelings and their accompanying behavioural manifestations. The client and the counsellor share responsibility for accomplishing this.

This therapeutic contract will be subject to review and renegotiation as considered necessary by either the client or the counsellor.

Client's signature . . . .

Date . . . .

Counsellor's signature . . . .

Date . . . .

Three-way contracts

Where a third party or an agency is involved in the referral, interim and final reports may be required as well as an audit of the work. The easiest way to clarify contracts with third parties is to make a three-way contract that sets out in explicit terms the rights and responsibilities of all parties, the client, the third party, and the counsellor.[6] It is useful to put this contract in writing, each party holding their own copy.

Example of a three-way contract

CONTRACT FOR COUNSELLING SERVICES

Between Dr P. Smith, General Practitioner, M. Williams, Counsellor, and A. Brown, Client.

The General Practitioner will:

1 refer the client to the counsellor
2 receive reports from the counsellor on work completed with the client within two weeks of completion
3 receive such interim reports as are deemed necessary either by the General Practitioner or by the Counsellor or by the Client
4 where appropriate, meet with the client and the counsellor together to discuss any relevant aspect of the work.

The Counsellor will:

1 assess the therapeutic needs of the client
2 inform the general practitioner if the client does not wish to enter counselling or if their needs cannot be met by the service provided
3 provide counselling sessions
4 give reasonable notice of any failure to attend wherever possible
5 provide such end and interim reports as are appropriate to the work undertaken
6 where appropriate, meet with the general practitioner and the client together to discuss any relevant aspect of the work.

The Client will:

1 attend appointments
2 give reasonable notice of inability to attend wherever possible
3 have the right to read any report written on them by the counsellor before it is sent to the general practitioner
4 have the right to include comment of their own on any report written on them by the counsellor
5 where appropriate, meet with the general practitioner and the counsellor together to discuss any relevant aspect of the work.

.... P Smith .... Date

.... M Williams .... Date

.... A Brown .... Date

Contracting issues

Open communication

Contracts such as those shown may seem unusual because of the extent of their openness. Open communication is an important principle of TA, and is one of the ways in which equal respect for all (I'm OK, you're OK) is practised. It helps stop *power plays*[7] and the keeping of secrets, and contributes to clear communication. This will help ensure that we establish the client's informed consent to the counselling process – an important ethical consideration.

Written or verbal contracts?

It has been suggested several times in the making of business and administrative contracts that this information might be written down for the client. However, many counsellors, especially those in independent practice, feel uncomfortable with written contracts, preferring instead to make verbal agreements with clients. Many clients feel similarly. It is not unusual for some clients to refuse to sign contracts. In such cases they often express the view that the counsellor is only interested in money or in protecting their own interests. Because of the discomfort that this type of challenge brings, a written contract might be avoided by the counsellor.

We need to be mindful that custom and practice in the counselling field are changing. Formal complaints and legal claims against counsellors are now part of what we have to learn to face and deal with in our profession. These changes, as well as good business practice and awareness of ethical principles such as informed consent, indicate that verbal agreements are becoming a thing of the past. I recommend written business and administrative contracts over verbal agreements for the following reasons:

◆ This ensures absolute clarity for all parties concerned.

◆ It offers some protection if the client or counsellor disagrees over the original contract agreement.

◆ Should the client bring a complaint against the counsellor, a written contract will specify and clarify the original agreements made.

◆ It sets out the boundaries of the relationship.

Keep your contracts simple, and if in doubt have them checked over by an expert.

Key skills

◆ Develop confidence and personal authority to specify the contract to the client.
◆ Be assertive and sensitive when you discuss the contract with your client.
◆ Discuss in supervision.

Exercise

1 Design a simple business contract that sets out your custom and practice.
2 With a partner, role play counsellor and client and introduce your business contract to the client in three scenarios.
3 Ask your partner to role play three types of client: (a) pleasing and accommodating (b) suspicious and hostile (c) passive.
4 Discuss the process and what you experienced.
5 Identify skills for further development.

Agreeing the contract

If the prospective client and counsellor are in agreement about the business and administrative details, the business meeting can be concluded and the therapeutic hour can commence. Where counsellor and client are not in agreement it is important to summarize the reasons for this and, if possible, to help the client identify the next course of action: seeking out a different kind of service, or a different kind of practitioner, and if necessary referring back to the initial referrer or agency.

Clients not suitable for TA counselling

Clients not suited to TA counselling are generally characterized by one or more of the following:

◆ unwillingness or inability to be self-reflective

◆ insufficient ability to contain their own feelings (people who 'slip and slide' through their own emotional world)

◆ a wish to be the passive recipient of help rather than an active and equal partner

◆ unwillingness to consider new perspectives or frames of reference

◆ unwillingness or inability to face further psychological pain as a necessary part of the healing process (such as grief or sadness)

◆ unwillingness to enter counselling, but present for some other reason such as at the suggestion of their general practitioner, or because of an ultimatum issued by a partner.

However, it is important to note that some clients may start out in this way, yet after two or three sessions may begin to move to a different attitude. It is only if they are steadfastly and rigidly fixed do we suggest that counselling is not likely to be helpful. Do not reject the person, only the approach.

The therapeutic contract

Therapeutic contracts were developed within the TA model. The concept has been widely borrowed, often without recognition of the fact. Making a therapeutic contract is one of the hallmarks of TA practice. Without a contract it is not TA. The TA counsellor uses the therapeutic contract as the focus of the work and will spend considerable time formulating a clear contract that can be easily remembered by both client and counsellor. This contract will be revisited and explored throughout the course of the counselling. As counselling progresses the contract is likely to be modified as new goals emerge.

Formulating the contract

TA counsellors use clear and simple language in formulating contracts that could be understood by a child. TA therapeutic contracts usually begin with an active statement such as 'I will'; the intention is to create the mindset for the client that they can take charge of their lives and their own process. In making the statement, like a positive affirmation, the goal is already in sight. The intention is that the client remembers the contract even when under stress. In taking time to formulate the contract, the process of the counselling is already under way.

An effective contract will include discussion and clarification of the following:[8]

◆ What is your goal in coming for counselling?

◆ How will you and I know when you have reached your goal?

◆ What might you have to let go of to reach your goal?

◆ What do you imagine will emerge in place of what you give up?

◆ How might you prevent yourself from reaching your goal?

◆ What part do you want me to play in helping you reach your goal?

When the therapeutic contract is about to be discussed for the first time, the point of changeover from the business meeting should be made quite clear to the client. A preliminary exploration of the therapeutic contract can then begin. After so much that has been concrete and factual, it is important to ease into a gentler style. It is the exceptional client who knows the exact nature of the therapeutic change they are seeking. Establishing a well-tailored contract can take several sessions; this is time well spent, because it allows the client to roam over their inner world until they reach a satisfactory understanding of their own wants and needs. Making a good therapeutic contract is not unlike tidying out a cupboard. Much will be discovered that needs reflecting on, reminiscing about, reorganizing, discarding or bringing out for use again.

Where a therapeutic contract is viable, some general agreement should have been reached about the focus for this by the end of the first meeting.

Case example: Angela

Angela, a slender woman in her mid twenties, described how she had rapidly gained promotion in the company she had joined immediately after leaving university. Her success was a surprise to her and a delight to her parents. She was the only one in the family to go to university; this in itself was a source of great pride to her parents. Her swift career success was 'icing on the cake' to them. Angela was embarrassed and felt uncomfortable about her parents' behaviour. They talked incessantly to friends and family, 'showing off' about her and ignoring her brother and sisters. She did not want to be singled out in this way. It was causing difficulties between her and her siblings; her success was more a matter of chance, 'being in the right place at the right time', than of merit. She felt she did not deserve such praise and found it embarrassing. Angela had managed to keep knowledge of her symptoms of panic and anxiety hidden from her parents: 'I couldn't take the hassle of them finding out.' She wanted to regain her composure and feel in control of herself.

Angela's difficulties appear to have some direct causes.

◆ the pressure she experiences due to parental praise
◆ her concern that rivalry and bad feeling are arising between her and her siblings
◆ her own view of her promotion as 'being in the right place at the right time'
◆ a belief that she is not particularly remarkable in her achievements.

Angela's desire to regain control is one that should be possible through counselling. What she wants matches with what the counsellor can reasonably expect to be able to help her achieve. An initial therapeutic contract can be agreed. After talking through the contract questions, Angela's therapeutic contract was agreed as 'I will relax and know what I want.'

Client–counsellor match

It is important to ensure that the client's problems and goals match the nature of the service on offer. Even when the business and administrative contracts have been agreed, it is still possible that a therapeutic contract may not be agreed. This possibility must be pointed out to the client at the start of the therapeutic time. There are many reasons why this may occur:

◆ The 'chemistry' between the counsellor and the client may be wrong.

◆ The client's goals and expectations cannot be met: for example, a client experiencing relationship difficulties wants to focus on their partner and not on themselves and their own part in the problem.

◆ The client may need a service the counsellor is unable to provide, such as extensive daily contact which is only possible in a residential or day-care setting.

◆ The client or counsellor might feel the difference between them is so great that it will diminish the effectiveness of the work and the relationship.

Examples

June visited a counsellor for one session and decided not to continue because 'the counsellor was too posh, she wouldn't understand my problems'.

Some counsellors feel they cannot work with some client problems because of personal beliefs. Anne, a committed Roman Catholic, considered that she was not the best person to work with people considering a termination. Age, gender, class and culture can be other factors that determine client/counsellor 'match'.

Key skills

◆ Ask the client how they experience you. What do they see as the differences between you? Once spoken about, many perceived 'differences' disappear.
◆ Be explicit with clients, giving a clear reason, if you decide not to go ahead and work with them.
◆ Think through what to say. You do not want to give the client the impression their need is beyond help. Avoid imposing your own beliefs on to the client. If unsure, discuss in supervision first.

Exercise

1 Examine your own belief system. What problems would you find difficulty in working with?
2 What 'unfinished business' do you bring into the counselling relationship that might affect the way you relate to specific client problems?
3 How might your age, gender, class or culture influence the way you view clients who are (a) similar to you (b) different to you?
4 Discuss with a colleague.

Summary

In this chapter we can appreciate just how much can be achieved in the first session. The counsellor has created a welcoming and sympathetic environment, adjusting her style of communication in order to attune to the client. In themselves, these skills are the fertile soil from which the counselling relationship will develop and deepen. Protection and containment provide a firm grounding for this relationship. We have explored how the counsellor can achieve this in the first session through clear contracting and a respectful relationship based on mutuality, which is the basis of sound ethical and professional practice.

In the next chapter we will look at how the relationship between counsellor and client deepens through the exploration of the client's story.

Many important key concepts have been introduced that will form the bedrock of your practice:

◆ rapport

◆ empathy

◆ presence

◆ reassurance

◆ complementary transaction

◆ ulterior transaction

◆ first transaction

◆ first few minutes

◆ positive stroke

- time structuring
- protection
- business contract
- administrative contract
- three-way contract
- therapeutic contract
- open communication
- power plays
- frame of reference.

We have looked at some key skills that will be important in all phases of counselling:

- explanation
- reassurance
- support.

Notes

1   'By the process of "empathy", the infant "prehends" the parental mood. If this mood is anxious or hostile, the infant directly prehends it as such, becomes itself uncomfortable quite as if it suffered bodily discomfort': R.L. Munro, *Schools of Psychoanalytic Thought* (Dryden, New York, 1955), p. 403.

2   E. Berne, *Principles of Group Treatment* (Grove, New York, 1966/78), Chapter 3, 'The First Three Minutes'.

3   E. Berne, *Sex in Human Loving* (Penguin, Harmondsworth, 1970/81), p. 192, 'The Six Hungers': 'One of the great problems in life is how to structure one's time, and this gives rise to a fifth kind of hunger . . . Structure hunger is more widespread and almost as damaging as malnutrition or malaria. When it becomes acute, it turns into incident hunger, which causes many people to get into trouble and make trouble just to relieve their boredom.'

4   E. Berne, *Principles*, p. 88.

5   I wish to acknowledge the suggestions about written contracts which were published in their journal by the then British Association for Counselling.

6   F. English, 'The three way contract', *Transactional Analysis Journal*, 5, 4 (1975), pp. 383–4.

7   C. Steiner, *Healing Alcoholism* (Grove, New York, 1979/81), p. 101: 'Cooperative relationships are based on the assumption that everyone has equal rights. They are best conducted in an atmosphere where power plays are not allowed, where people do not keep secrets from each other.'

8   A number of authors give their own version of contract questions. See: M.M. Holloway and W.H. Holloway, *The Contract Setting Process* (Midwest Institute for Human Understanding, Medina, OH, 1973), p. 35; M. James, 'Treatment Procedure', in *Techniques in Transactional Analysis* (Addison-Wesley, Reading, MA, 1977), pp. 106–7.

Further reading

Contracts

Loomis, M. (1982) 'Contracting for change', *Transactional Analysis Journal*, 12 (1), pp. 51–5.

Transactions

Berne, E. (1964/1985) *Games People Play.* Harmondsworth: Penguin. Chapter 2, 'Transactional Analysis'.

The first three minutes

Berne, E. (1966/1978) *Principles of Group Treatment.* New York: Grove. Chapter 3, 'The First Three Minutes'.

The stroke economy

Steiner, C. (1981) *The Other Side of Power.* New York: Grove. pp. 88–9, 'The Stroke Economy'.

Time structuring

Berne, E. (1972/1987) *What Do You Say After You Say Hello?* London: Corgi. pp. 21–5, 'Time Structuring'.

3 · Building the Relationship and Analysing the Client's Internal World

The relationship with your client has begun. It is very new and in need of sensitive and careful attention so that it can be strengthened and developed. As you enter this next stage of work your main goals with your client are to:

♦ build on and strengthen the relationship by tuning into their inner world

♦ help them describe their difficulties in more detail

♦ tell their story

♦ analyse their internal world

♦ show that you are impacted by their internal reality

♦ instil hope that change is possible.

The key outcomes you can expect are:

♦ a stronger therapeutic alliance

♦ an understanding of your client's ego image and ego state structure, stroke pattern and time structure

♦ your client's Child feels heard and protected, their Parent feels understood, and their Adult feels recognized as the window on reality

♦ your client feels sufficient trust in you and what you offer to believe change is possible.

Finding out more

Helping your client tune into their internal world

In this early phase, which usually begins in the second or third session, it is important to help your client tune in more closely to their internal world and their felt experience. For some clients their inner world is a familiar and frequently visited place. For others it is frightening and alien territory which, in itself, evokes unease. With each new client you need to assess levels of anxiety at starting this inner journey, adapting your approach to fit individual need. A good way to do this is by continuing to use *complementary transactions* in order to build on your client's first experience of you. Your style and approach must feel familiar. Your client wants to feel that you are available to them in the way that they need (that the ego state they address in you is the ego state from which you respond). This builds security and helps to establish continuity in the relationship.

Questioning

To help expand and explore the presenting problem the counselling approach needs to include sensitive questioning about the client's experience. Questions need to be open-ended and general so that they help your client explore the peaks, valleys and plateaux of their inner world, becoming increasingly familiar with its terrain.

This method of inquiry is important for the TA counsellor because in TA we are concerned with how the past (the content of the Child and Parent ego states) influences the present Adult reality.

Example
◆ What was it like living so far away from home?
◆ How did you feel inside when you were told that you were adopted?

In general, 'what' and 'how' questions enable exploration of the inner world. 'When' and 'why' questions require specific information that inhibits the process of exploration and tends to stop an open and general searching of the inner world. Questions such as 'Why did you live so far away from home?' or 'When did you find out that you were adopted?' do little to encourage self-exploration and tend to result in brief responses dominated by facts. However, they are sometimes necessary when you want to ascertain important information. Questions form part of the doorway into the inner world; they are a potent tool by which the TA counsellor hopes to inquire further into hitherto unrevealed aspects of the client's experience. They are not an end in themselves and should not dominate, otherwise the client may feel unhelpfully interrogated.

A common pitfall: blocking by the Parent ego state

The client's Parent ego state may attempt to block the exploration of her thoughts and feelings. It is very important that at this stage the counsellor recognizes and acknowledges the Parent through the use of complementary transactions. A common pitfall is that the Parent in the counsellor might begin to battle with the Parent of the client in terms of who is going to control the session.

Example

During the early phase of gathering information, Philip, a financial adviser, expressed considerable anxiety about his future: 'I'm frightened about my old age and whether I will have enough money to live.'

As the counsellor began to question him more closely, asking about his current financial situation, he suddenly pulled up a psychological drawbridge shutting the counsellor out: 'How rude of you, this topic is definitely off the agenda!' Taken aback, the counsellor reacted from an over-controlling Parent ego state: 'You must trust me and be willing to answer personal questions, otherwise there is no point in you being here.'

Counsellor and client were battling about who was in charge of the process. This exchange set back the trust that was building in the relationship. The counsellor had to work hard to re-establish the equilibrium. Fortunately she was immediately aware of her shift into Parent and was able to retrieve the situation.

Showing you understand: bull's-eye transaction

The bull's-eye transaction is one of the most useful transactions in helping your client to feel understood.[1] It allows you to demonstrate your ability to tune into your client by responding to all three ego states with one transaction. A bull's-eye transaction is one statement that addresses all three ego states. Using a bull's-eye increases your client's experience of your presence. Overall your client feels that you are fine tuning to their felt experience, working with exquisite sensitivity to decode and understand their inner reality. This transaction is illustrated in Figure 3.1.

Example: bull's-eye transaction 1

I can see you are anxious,	*Adult to Child*
and that you want to keep your privacy,	*Adult to Parent*
many people feel this way in counselling when	
they first begin to talk about intimate matters.	*Adult to Adult*

In this example, the counsellor is recognizing the client's fear (A–C: stimulus to Child (SC) in Figure 3.1), acknowledging their reluctance to discuss the cause (A–P: stimulus to Parent (SP), and appealing to the client's Adult (A–A: stimulus to Adult (SA)) to mediate between Child and Parent by normalizing discomfort as something many people sponta-

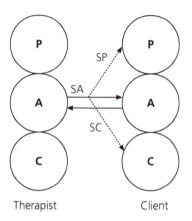

Figure 3.1 Bull's-eye transaction

Reprinted with permission from Stan Woollams. *Transactional Analysis*. Dexter, MI: Huron Valley Institute Press.

neously experience when first talking about intimate things. The transaction is aimed at dissolving the client's internal conflict ('I want to talk' (Child) versus 'you mustn't' (Parent)) and helping them to find a solution acceptable to both Parent and Child ('talking is a good idea, it's part of the healing' (Adult)).

With a bull's-eye there are no hard and fast rules about whether to address the Child or Parent first; the decision is entirely dependent on your assessment of which ego state it is better to address first. It is, however, important to make the final statement to the client's Adult so that neither Parent nor Child has the last word. The Adult is asked to take charge and figure out a solution acceptable to both.

Example: bull's-eye transaction 2

I can see you are upset,	*Adult to Child*
and that you don't want to show weakness,	*Adult to Parent*
many people cry when they first recall painful memories.	*Adult to Adult*

In this example, the counsellor is recognizing the client's distress (A–C: SC), acknowledging their reluctance to express it (A–P: SP), and appealing to the client's Adult (A–A: SA) to mediate between Child and Parent by normalizing crying as something many people spontaneously experience when first talking about painful things. The transaction is aimed at dissolving the client's internal conflict ('I want to cry' (Child) versus 'you mustn't' (Parent)) and helping them to find a solution acceptable to both Parent and Child ('crying is a good idea, it's part of the healing' (Adult)).

Case example: Angela
Showing understanding

Angela's second session

At her second visit, Angela seemed very tense, as if she were making a great effort to remain outwardly calm. Her hands were tightly clenched in her lap and she occasionally bit her lip as she talked, as if trying to clamp down her words. Although her Adult was in charge it was clear that at any moment her distressed Child threatened to overwhelm her.

Adult-to-Adult complementary transactions

Angela's contract specified her desire to feel appropriately in charge of herself. It was important to support her in this and help her strengthen the ease with which she could do so. Recognizing the rightness of helping Angela stay in Adult, her counsellor decided on Adult–Adult complementary transactions. Seeing someone so distressed evoked in the counsellor a strong temptation to respond from a Nurturing Parent ego state. This would be an error. It would have the effect of weakening Angela's Adult functioning and inviting her Child to take a central role. Angela needed experience of her effective Adult self, not the Child turmoil that she found so debilitating.

The counsellor's reflections

This would be an important area to follow. The counsellor made a mental note of her own response of wanting to mother Angela. This raised some self-supervisory questions to reflect on after the session:

◆ Do people tend to respond to Angela from Nurturing Parent?
◆ Does her Adult get decommissioned?

This would be an important area to follow up at a later time after understanding the significance of her own response and its part in Angela's story.

How the session progressed

The session began like this:

Counsellor: It's good to see you today.	Greeting. Stroke (A).
Angela: Hi.	Response (A).
Counsellor: Have you had any thoughts about our last meeting?	Questioning to allow feedback (A).

Angela: No, not really.	Curtailing exploration (A). The brevity of response doesn't fit with the ulterior communication of barely contained distress noted earlier and conveyed by expression and gesture.
Counsellor: Sometimes, at the start of counselling, we can feel as if the floodgates will give way at any moment.	Bull's-eye (A–C) recognizing the Child's feeling of being overwhelmed, communicated at the ulterior level, with gesture and facial expression.
Holding on tightly can seem like the only choice.	Bull's-eye (A–P) acknowledging the good sense of the Parent approach communicated at the ulterior level, with gesture and facial expression.
It is important to stay in charge whilst slowly exploring those matters that are causing difficulty.	Bull's-eye (A–A) supporting the Adult role and giving permission to proceed at a manageable pace which takes account of the Child's fear and suggests a better method than the Parent's choice.
Angela: Do you think this will work?	Angela reveals her fear in the guise of an Adult question, already following up the counsellor's suggestion from the bull's-eye. It is a direct request for reassurance made in a new way (A).
Counsellor: Whilst there are no guarantees, I think you will begin to understand the cause of your difficulties and find a solution that feels right for you.	Reassurance is given by describing the two-stage process of understanding and solution. The counsellor avoids promising the Child a guarantee and describes to the Adult its central role.
When did you first notice the problem?	A closed question designed to bridge with the counsellor's last statement and help the client begin the process of recall by fixing the time frame (A).
Angela: It was about six months ago. I started to feel sick when I drove into the office. At first I didn't take much notice, I thought I was coming down with something.	Important factual information is given about the initial nature of the problem and Angela's reaction (A).

Counsellor: When did you realize there was more to it?	A second closed question to fix Angela's identification of the problem (A).
Angela: Well the symptoms got worse, sweating, that kind of thing, and they only happened around work. I knew that must be significant.	Angela expands on what she has noticed and when she decided it was significant (A).
Counsellor: What did you make of this experience?	Now that two crucial markers are in place, when and what, the counsellor invites Angela to begin a more free-ranging exploration (A).

Telling the story

Developing phenomenological recall

As the work progresses your focus should be on helping your client to identify relevant aspects of their own story or history. This may take several sessions. The depth and range of the recall should be decided by you and your client together so that the contract is clear and the client has given consent. As a general rule, do not initiate exploration of non-essential areas; this can have the effect of unbinding experiences that are not directly connected with the problem.

Unbinding

Unbinding is the freeing of emotional energy which is currently 'locked' or stored away in an ego state.[2] This energy might be consciously or unconsciously blocked and can be unwittingly accessed by a counsellor using invasive techniques. Unwelcome memories, emotional pain and hidden aspects of the personality can be released. At this early stage the relationship is unlikely to have a secure enough base for a client to deal with such highly charged material.

Unbinding emotional energy creates unnecessary vulnerability which not only has a destabilizing effect but requires additional therapeutic time to resolve. As we saw with Philip, the client unwilling to talk about money, sometimes the counsellor does this unintentionally when something unexpected is uncovered, or the client themselves spontaneously opens up something. Where this happens a decision will have to be made as to whether it is possible to rebind the material without any harmful effect or whether it is necessary to incorporate it into the work.

In telling the story, both past and present aspects need inclusion. Key events, people, outcomes and decisions are explored, together with the emotional content. Clients are helped to recall their experiences by focusing on context, the what, when and how of the circumstances.[3] It is important to remember that the client's story is their remembered and interpreted recall of themselves and their lives. It may not be factually accurate in all respects. By and large this does not matter because the counsellor is working with felt reality and perceived truth. Whatever any of us recalls may be subject to forgetting, embellishment or a change of focus. This is normal. By helping clients reinstate context they are able to recall their felt experience with greater clarity.

Case example: Angela
The problem and the family script

Angela described her dawning awareness that her problems around work were likely to be psychological in origin. The notion horrified her. Her family valued stoicism and exemplified a 'no-nonsense, get-on-with-it approach' to managing their own lives, an approach which Angela herself had taken on. Seeking psychological help was outside the family script. Psychological problems were not considered real and therefore psychological help was deemed unnecessary.

Her parents' stories in context

On inquiring further into her parents' stories the counsellor learned that Angela's father was the oldest son of a large family living in a coal mining community. The family had had to eke out a living. Her father had left school at a young age to provide an extra wage for the family. As a child he had displayed some musical ability and had dreamed of a musical career. He took his dashed dreams and his appointed lot in life in good part, proud to help his family. His musical abilities eventually found an outlet playing the trumpet in the colliery band.

Angela's mother was the only daughter of a cleric father and a mother who worked tirelessly in the parish. Her parents had been unable to have any more children and adored their daughter.

Angela's parents met at a dance and romance quickly blossomed. Angela's eldest sister was conceived and the couple, although impelled to marry by their respective families because of the pregnancy, did so happily enough. The only clouds on the horizon were the guilt Angela's mother felt at letting down her family who had had higher expectations for her; and Angela's father's anxiety about how his own family would manage without his wage. Neither family voiced any disquiet to their respective children.

Angela's response

In recounting what she knew of her parents' history, Angela became silent and reflective several times. At the point where she described their marriage her eyes filled with soft tears which rolled gently down her cheeks. She voiced no spoken comment.

Angela's birth

As the impact of her recall of her parents' stories began to wane, the counsellor asked Angela to continue. She described the birth of her three older siblings happening in quick succession. Ten years later Angela came along, 'an accident' as her mother had once put it. Angela became silent for well over a minute. The counsellor gently inquired what it was like to be described as 'an accident'. Angela didn't respond directly to the question. Instead she took and held a deep breath, paused again, looked up and met the counsellor's gaze. 'They wanted her to get rid of me.' She sobbed deeply.

Angela's mother had told her that her paternal grandfather had advised his son against having a fourth child. His reasoning was pragmatic. The family were just emerging from 10 years of babies and financial hardship. For the first time money problems were abating. Angela's mother had never found pregnancy and childbirth easy and her physical health was not always robust. For whatever reason the family ignored this advice and knuckled down to providing for a fourth child.

Angela's childhood

With an age gap of so many years between Angela and her siblings, she quickly became the eternal baby of the family. All her childhood stories describe her as a sunny-natured, lively child, adored by everyone. As she pondered on what she had described, Angela made a telling comment: 'I always felt I had so much to make up for. My parents worked hard and sacrificed so much to give me the best.'

By the time she entered secondary school, the family were better off. They had moved to a nearby town where both parents found employment in a factory, working overtime whenever they could. They decided to send her to a private school. Academically she did well at school; her natural aptitude clearly thrilled her parents. Socially, however, she felt 'one down'. She did not feel as good as the other girls who came from families with a higher social status than her own. Angela often felt 'nauseous and anxious' on her way to school but 'buckled down' to her studies because she did not want to fail her parents. By the time she reached 15 it was understood that she was studying to enter university. Angela commented: 'It's funny, I can't remember anyone ever talking about it. It was just decided. I never even thought about not going.'

Analysing the client's story

Assessing a client's story is important. It gives the counsellor a structured and consistent way to reconsider what has been shared and to sift through and analyse the material.

The ego image

Starting with an ego image of the client is always valuable.[4] An ego image is the impression the client conveys of their active child ego state. It is communicated through posture, gesture, expression and voice tone. Hairstyle and way of dressing, even the job they do, will provide further clues. An ego image is the crystallization of this impression made by using *intuition*.[5] Drawing into awareness the overall or dominant impression conveyed by the client is extremely helpful in stepping back from the interaction with the client and reviewing how we have been impacted. Most of us do this from time to time when we make comments such as, 'He's just a big baby', 'She spat her dummy out', 'They're like a couple of teenagers.'

Developing and using intuitive abilities comes more easily to some than others and is partly a matter of temperament. As Luke Skywalker, the hero of the classic film *Star Wars*, found, it is partly a matter of practise and partly a matter of faith in our own perceptions. Using intuitive perceptions is akin to deliberately allowing our vision to become blurred so that everything goes slightly out of focus. In the process, new and sometimes surprising images can emerge with greater clarity.

The ego image can be strengthened when the counsellor pays careful attention to her own internal and behavioural response to the client. In formulating an ego image of Angela, her counsellor began to understand her earlier desire to nurture her. The counsellor's image of Angela was of a tense and anxious child trying very hard not to have wants and needs, but who really wanted to curl up in a warm lap and feel reassured. Although she had been the family 'baby', Angela lacked sufficient experience of unconditional loving. Linking this image with the stories of hardship endured by Angela's parents created a wider picture, one in which at least two generations had missed out on some of the tenderness which would have strengthened their ability to trust their own wants and needs without becoming anxious and tense. The counsellor concluded that Angela's present difficulties were partly rooted in her family's history. She was experiencing family script symptoms in her own personal and unique way.

> **Exercise**
> **Developing skills in analysing the client's story**
> 1 Explore your client's life story, asking about:
>   ◆ mother's story
>   ◆ father's story
>   ◆ the story of the client's birth, childhood, and relationship with their siblings.
> 2 Formulate an ego image and reflect on what this tells you about your client.

Ego state structure

Structural ego states describe psychological makeup and personality structure.[6] They show how the content of each has evolved. By contrast (as we saw in Chapter 2) functional ego states describe how ego states are used. Mapping the client's structural ego states allows the counsellor to begin understanding the sense the client has made of their experience and how they have formulated it. In addition it facilitates understanding of how transgenerational experience, or family history, is passed down from parent to child.

The model is shown in Figure 3.2. The three domains are as follows:

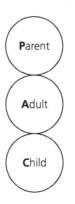

Figure 3.2 Structural ego state model

◆ *Parent* Unresolved thoughts, feelings and behaviours introjected (taken without question) from significant others.

- *Adult* Thoughts, feelings and behaviours consonant with current, consensual reality.

- *Child* Unfinished business 'relics'[7] of the person's past unresolved thoughts, feelings and behaviours deriving directly from their past experiences; not limited to childhood, but extending to the whole of the person's past life.

Case example: Angela
Ego state structure

Angela's counsellor focused on the following areas:

- what Angela had introjected (taken without question) from her parents' feelings, attitudes and behaviours (but also including anything from siblings old enough to have been perceived in a parenting role) (Parent)
- what she had derived from her past direct experience which was still unresolved and inappropriate to the here-and-now (Child)
- her current feelings, attitudes and behaviours that were in accord with here-and-now reality (Adult).

Angela's ego state structure is illustrated in Figure 3.3. Her ego states can be summarized as follows:

- *Parent* Duty comes before pleasure; always put other people first; self-sacrifice requires some personal suffering.
- *Adult* The symptoms I'm experiencing are not just physiological; I want to change my job, but I can't find a way to do it; I feel stuck, helpless and afraid.
- *Child* I am the apple of their eye; I have to make up for their suffering; I am talented and can make them feel better.

Analysis of Angela's ego state structure

By mapping the structure of Angela's ego states, the counsellor began to form a clear picture of her script. This may be summarized as:

Virtue is to be found in hard work, diligence and self-sacrifice.

Angela achieved this by sublimating her individual wants and needs. Her panic and anxiety stem from the conflict created by the message 'you are special' on the one hand, and the overriding family script to be strong and accept your lot in life on the other.

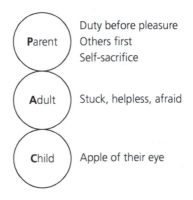

Figure 3.3 Angela's ego state structure

Reprinted with permission from Souvenir Press Ltd. Eric Berne (1961) *Transactional Analysis in Psychotherapy*. London: Souvenir Press

'How do we get to feel good?': analysing stroke patterns

> How do we get to feel good? If people rub your back or smile and say 'Hi', they are giving you strokes. Strokes are what people do or say to other people to make them feel good.[8]

We learn our original stroke pattern in childhood through our family and culture. Our family shows us what we have to do so that they will feel like 'rubbing our back' and making us feel good. As adults we transport this pattern of seeking strokes into our lives and our relationships. As counsellors, an important part of learning to understand our clients is to find out how they keep themselves feeling good with strokes.

What are strokes?

To be psychologically healthy, we all need

◆ stimulation – circumstances and experiences that keep us feeling our life is interesting and meaningful

◆ recognition of who we are and what we do

◆ emotional and physical contact with others.

Collectively, these are described as the need for strokes.[9] Strokes may be:

◆ positive (they make us feel good) or negative (they make us feel bad)

◆ conditional (based on an action) or unconditional (strokes about being).

Our *stroke balance*[10] is an estimation of the positive and negative, conditional and unconditional strokes which we seek out. It tells us about the kinds of strokes which make us comfortable; those which we find uncomfortable; those of which we have an abundance; and those which are in short supply. By inference, it reveals a lot about how we function in our world and the kind of relationships we seek out.

Case example: Angela's stroke pattern

For Angela to begin to take account of her individual needs it is important that she understands how she finds and uses strokes and the links with family scripting. Angela's family history demonstrates that economic survival necessitated giving conditional strokes for actions that furthered the well-being of the family. For example, her father felt recognized for starting work at a young age to help the family, rather than following his own dreams. Angela describes many examples of the conditional positive stroking she has received: for being a 'sunny-natured' child, for being the youngest (gifts from her siblings), and for being the first person to attend university. These are the conditions she has to fulfil to 'get her back rubbed and be made to feel good'. These conditional strokes bring Angela stimulation, recognition and emotional closeness with the family.

Overall, Angela's stroke balance tends towards the positive conditional. As she develops her relationship with her counsellor, she will probably try to establish similar patterns of stroking because this is how she experiences closeness. Her counsellor will need to respond with care and sensitivity, giving Angela enough of the strokes she needs so that she feels good about herself. As counselling progresses, her counsellor will gradually shift the ways in which she strokes Angela and move towards unconditional stroking. Changing patterns of stroking is not easy. We all cling to what we know works for us. Changing this needs to be done slowly and carefully.

Analysing time structuring

To ensure our stroke needs are met, we have to structure our time in ways that will provide opportunities for receiving the kinds of strokes we need.[11] Time can be structured in a variety of ways:

1 *Withdrawal* Literally withdrawing from proximity with others and spending time alone, or whilst being with other people remaining withdrawn and out of contact. Interpersonally, risk of hurt (feeling bad) is minimal, but becoming stroke deprived is a real possibility if we withdraw for too long.

2 *Rituals* Ritualized exchanges that contain a high degree of social predictability ('Hi! Nice day', 'Yes, isn't it'). Or highly ritualized social activities with no spontaneous social exchange. There is minimal risk of hurt. We receive low-impact, predictable strokes.

3 *Pastimes* Discussing favourite topics such as food, fashion, music. Again the element of predictability of the exchange and therefore the safety of it is still high. Strokes are more meaningful, but still not high impact.

4 *Activities* Goal oriented tasks where outcomes matter and we are assessed on the basis of our abilities. Work is the main activity for most adults. Here the element of predictability lessens and the risks increase. As a result, strokes are felt more intensely and carry more impact, either positively or negatively.

5 *Psychological games* Repetitive interactions with others where outcomes are predictably negative in stroking terms. For example, 'Why don't you try . . .?', 'Yes, I thought of that but it won't work because . . .' (both people end up feeling useless). These exchanges are repeated until one of the players concludes the exchange is going nowhere. They both end up feeling unrecognized by the other and negatively stroked.

6 *Intimacy* Opening ourselves to emotional closeness, love or, if things go wrong, rejection. Allowing our vulnerabilities to be exposed with someone who matters. The risks are high and consequently these strokes have maximum impact.

To summarize the discussion on time structuring and stroke yield:

♦ Withdrawal results in no external strokes and reliance on internal ones.

♦ Rituals provide a few safe, low-level strokes.

♦ Pastimes give a higher yield of safe, predictable strokes.

♦ Activities give strokes that are unpredictable. They may be positive or negative depending on performance.

♦ Games provide a predictably high yield of negative strokes.

♦ Intimacy can yield high-octane positive strokes or negative strokes that taste like a poisoned chalice.

Case example: Angela
Analysis of her time structure

Angela has focused on activity as one of her key ways of structuring time. By working hard and being successful she ensures positive conditional strokes. She is concerned that her source of these types of strokes will dry up if she reveals her difficulties. If her family and colleagues fail to deliver the usual yield of positive conditional strokes, she anticipates a loss of their esteem and a consequent drop in her own self-esteem. She is understandably anxious about this. Her self-stroking for her work performance has already shifted from a positive to a negative one.

   Her counsellor infers that Angela spends a lot of time with her family pastiming about her work accomplishments and gaining positive strokes for this. Of equal import is Angela's lack of any mention of other significant ways of structuring time with non-family members. She does not seem to have friends or interests outside work. Is Angela overly reliant on her family as her main social group, with whom she spends time and from whom she receives strokes? This will need further consideration as the counselling progresses.

Our search for familiar strokes through time structuring leads us into the taking of familiar roles which, as we shall see in the next chapter, leads to psychological games.

Some commonly asked questions

How much theory should I share with clients?

The whole philosophical base of TA is based on equality of relationship and the sharing of information. This does not mean that we burden our clients with reams of theory that may bore or confuse them, or which they could use as a means to talk about themselves rather than experience their emotional pain.

   There are times when it is genuinely useful to share something theoretical with a client, and times when it is not. Share information if it is likely to result in:

◆ a strengthened Adult

◆ the client's increased understanding and awareness

◆ the client being more willing to experience and explore their emotional responses.

Do not share information if:

- you are doing so because you find the theory fascinating or it makes you feel good

- it will confuse your client

- this will enable your client to avoid experiencing their emotions

- you are stuck and can't think of anything else to do.

Can the use of so many techniques inhibit the therapeutic relationship?

Sometimes, counsellors new to TA worry that with such a cornucopia of techniques to draw on, the relationship will get lost. Techniques serve merely as a vehicle for progressing the work. They are a means to an end and not an end in themselves. Through them you show your client care, concern and exquisite attention, journeying with her into her internal world. She begins to sense your presence, to feel less on her own with her difficulties and more hopeful that you can help her make changes. Of course, as with any intervention, an insensitive approach can create distance in the relationship. But this is a matter of personal style, not a fault of technique. The more you practise, the more familiar and at ease you will feel with the techniques, until they become second nature to you. Your client will take her cue from you. If you are open, contactful and present she will sense this irrespective of the 'what' of your approach. Equally, if you are withdrawn and focused on methodology ('counting time') and not on the relationship, she will know this.

Summary

In this chapter we have looked at ways of building and consolidating the counselling relationship through developing counsellor presence and facilitating the client to tell her story and increase emotional recall of significant life events. The counsellor has made an analysis of her client's ego state structure, stroke balance and ways of structuring time in order to build her understanding of her client.

Key concepts that have been considered include:

- ego image

- unbinding

- structural ego state

- stroke balance

- time structure

Key skills we have used are:

◆ complementary transactions

◆ questioning

◆ bull's-eye transaction

◆ creating an ego image

◆ ego state analysis

◆ analysing stroke balance

◆ analysing time structure.

Exercises

3.1 From a television soap opera, novel or film, select a character.
   (a) Decide on the key features of their story.
   (b) Make a provisional assessment of their ego image, structural ego state, stroke balance, time structuring, roles taken and family games, key script choices and script matrix, and key permissions.
   (c) With a partner, share your view of the story and TA assessment.
   (d) Partner gives feedback on your assessment.

3.2 (a) Partner to role play the character who is seeking counselling from you.
   (b) Practise using bull's-eye transactions.

3.3 Continue the role play:
   (a) Partner gives feedback on how you came across.
   (b) Practise specifying the key points of the story.
   (c) Partner gives feedback on how you came across.
   (d) Give yourself strokes for what you did well.
   (e) Make a note of your learning needs and, together with your partner, specify goals for developing expertise.

Notes

1   E. Berne, *Transactional Analysis in Psychotherapy* (Souvenir, London, 1961/1980), p. 236: 'The ideal intervention is the "bull's eye", one which is meaningful and acceptable to all three aspects of the patient's personality, since all three overhear everything that is said.'

2   Ibid., pp. 40–1.

3   'Bearing in mind context dependency, we can improve clients' recall if we encourage

them to reinstate the context as fully as possible': J. McNamara and C. Lister-Ford, 'Ego states and the psychology of memory', *Transactional Analysis Journal*, 25, 2 (1995), p. 144.

4   '"Ego images" . . . are specific perceptions of the patient's active archaic ego state in relation to the people around him': E. Berne, *Intuition and Ego States* (TA Press, San Francisco, 1977), p. 102.

5   'Intuition is knowledge based on experience and acquired through sensory contact with the subject without the "intuiter" being able to formulate to himself or to others exactly how he came to his conclusions': ibid., p. 4.

6   An ego state 'is a system of feelings accompanied by a related set of behaviour patterns . . . [These are] psychological realities . . . [Ego states] can be sorted into the following categories: (1) ego states which resemble those of parental figures; (2) ego states which are autonomously directed towards objective appraisal of reality and (3) those which represent archaic relics': E. Berne, *Games People Play* (Penguin, Harmondsworth, 1964/1985), p. 23.

7   'The Child ego state is a set of feelings, attitudes, and behaviour patterns which are relics of the individual's own childhood': Berne, *Transactional Analysis*, p. 77.

8   A.M. Freed, *T.A. for Tots (and Other Prinzes)* (Jalmar, Rolling Hills, CA, 1973/86), pp. 62–3.

9   E. Berne, *Sex in Human Loving* (Penguin, Harmondsworth, 1970/1981), pp. 191–2.

10   'Children are controlled by regulating their stroke input, and grownups work and respond to societal demands in order to get strokes': C. Steiner, *Scripts People Live* (Bantam, New York, 1974/1982), p. 135.

11   'The eternal problem of the human being is how to structure his waking hours . . . Structure hunger has . . . survival value . . . to avoid sensory and emotional starvation': Berne, *Games People Play*, pp. 15–19.

Further reading

Bull's-eye transaction

Woollams, S. and Brown, M. (1978) *Transactional Analysis.* Ann Arbor, MI: Huron Valley Institute Press. Chapter 4, pp. 76–7.

Ego states

Clarkson, P. and Gilbert, M. (1988) 'Berne's original model of ego states: some theoretical considerations', *Transactional Analysis Journal*, 18 (1): 20–9.

4 · Developing the Relationship and Completing Analysis of the Client's Internal World

You and your client have now established a secure and trusting base for your working relationship. In this chapter we will look at how you deepen your relationship with your client, as well as deepening the client's own relationship with their inner Child. The working relationship is still tenuous. These are 'early days', and you need to continue to tread with care and sensitivity. This next stage will involve some gentle challenging as the client develops awareness and begins to see things in their own behaviour which they do not like or which they want to avoid. They will also begin to see their relationships in a new light. These revelations can be uncomfortable or even painful. In your counselling you need to keep a delicate balance between empathic attunement and heightening new awareness.

Key goals are to:

◆ complete your analysis of your client's internal world

◆ specify key script features

◆ develop the relationship by demonstrating your skill and sensitivity in helping your client to face important realizations about their script story.

As these goals are realized a number of developments will occur:

◆ You will have a more complete picture of the relevant features of your client's internal world.

◆ You and your client will reach an informed agreement about what needs to be worked through to realize the goals of the counselling.

◆ Your working relationship with the client will come to a crossroads: can script issues be faced and worked with?

Completing analysis of the client's story

Analysing the key psychological game

The next step is to analyse the key psychological game (or games, if there is more than one) in your client's script. This game keeps the client locked in script.

Definition of a psychological game

> A game is an ongoing series of complementary ulterior transactions progressing to a well-defined, predictable outcome ... it is a recurring set of transactions, often repetitious, superficially plausible, with a concealed motivation.[1]

A psychological game is the script in action, or to put it another way, script is progressed through playing psychological games. Games are characterized by three features:

♦ their ulterior and manipulative qualities

♦ the switch in ego states of at least one player which reveals the real motivation behind the game

♦ the bad outcome or 'payoff' at the end.

When you are first thinking about games, analysing the roles of the main people in your client's story (including your client, of course) using the drama triangle[2] is a straightforward and effective way of gaining immediate insight into how the drama of the game operates. When people take on these roles they give up their autonomy in favour of assuming family roles[3] in script dramas that are repetitious and predictable and lead, over and over again, to the same inevitable outcomes.

Analysing roles on the drama triangle

> Only three roles are necessary in drama analysis to depict ... emotional reversals. These action roles ... are the Persecutor, Rescuer and Victim. Drama begins when these roles are established ... There is no drama unless there is a switch in the roles.[4]

The positions on the drama triangle are shown in Figure 4.1. The roles are as follows:

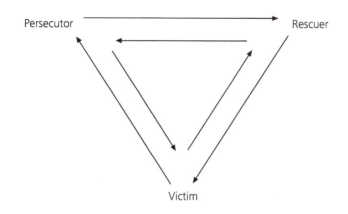

Figure 4.1 Drama triangle and action roles

The drama triangle was originally published in 'Fairy Tales and Script Drama Analysis' by Stephen B. Karpman, MD, in the *Transactional Analysis Bulletin*, Volume 7 (26), pp. 39–43, 1968. Reprinted here with permission of Stephen B. Karpman and the International Transactional Analysis Association.

◆ The rescuer is doing more for somebody else than that person is doing for themselves, even though they are capable of doing it; or he is doing so much for somebody else that it is detrimental to his own circumstances; or both.

◆ The persecutor is deliberately and systematically controlling, harassing or punishing someone.

◆ The victim is behaving in a disempowered, one-down way.

Case example: Angela

The family drama

Angela's story describes family members rescuing and persecuting each other over at least two generations. Her father rescued his parents, relinquishing his own dreams, and going to work in order to bring in extra income. His family may well not have been able to do more for themselves by way of bringing in extra income. But his choice was certainly not beneficial to his own circumstances and he himself ends up as a victim of his own decisions by living in financially impoverished circumstances, unable to find full outlet for his creativity.

How Angela is playing the game

Angela is rescuing her own family by living out their dreams in an unquestioning way, allowing them to vicariously experience the pleasure of choices they themselves felt unable to make. Remember her telling comment about university, 'It was just decided. I never even thought about not going.' It is as if she is describing a dream-like state in which she hypnotically follows the well-trodden family path of being 'happy to help'.[5] Whilst her father pleased his own family, her mother disappointed hers and felt eternally guilty. Angela seems caught in the nub of the combined conflict of her parents. At the present she is just about hanging on to a situation that assures her of pleasing them, but she is now starting to feel a victim of her choices through her symptoms. If she cannot solve her difficulties without their knowledge she risks moving into an arena where they are not so well pleased and, in time, may even come to be displeased. Since Angela has made career choices based on her original unquestioning decision about taking a university course, it is likely that she will come to the point where she will need to question these original choices and the bases on which they were made. In such circumstances she could well find herself deep in the midst of the historical dilemmas of her own parents – to continue to please in order to try to make amends for all that has disappointed her family over the years, or to make autonomous choices where she risks disappointing her family.

The family game dynamics are clearly seen from the position taken by the protagonist in each of the last two generations of Angela's story: they are rescuers to others in the family whom they perceive as needy victims. Through the act of rescuing they eventually place themselves in a victim position. The role of persecutor is subtly played out. Family members systematically control each other by making choices and doing what they believe 'is best' for the other person: for example, sending Angela to a school that she was ill equipped to deal with, and 'deciding' that she should go to university.

Identifying games

Identifying a game is simply a matter of becoming familiar with the different games,[6] drawing up a list of possibilities and, during the counselling process, eliminating those that do not fit. This leaves those that do. Sometimes there is more than one main game. The main game Angela describes is 'happy to help', a so-called 'good'[7] game because it can have positive social consequences as in Angela's family, where in truth the family has been helped to thrive by the sacrifices of individual members. However, the current generation no longer needs this kind of sacrifice. Family circumstances, the social context and work opportunities have moved on since Angela's parents were children. Angela no longer needs to play the familial game in order for her family to survive.

Angela has gained considerable insight. She is now ready to move on and look at her script choices.

Analysing key script choices

What is script?

> [Script is] an ongoing program developed in early childhood under parental influence which directs the individual's behaviour in the most important aspects of . . . life.[8]

Scripts are transgenerational; they are passed down from one generation to the next. They are the vehicle for passing on family traditions, knowledge, beliefs, attitudes and aspirations. They are coercive, demanding adaptation and compliance in favour of free choice so that family culture is preserved and passed between the generations. Our script defines the major turning points in our life and the outcomes that will result.

How are scripts passed on?

Here are some of the most important ways:

1 Non-verbally:

- ◆ *Stroking* How the child is made to feel good or bad by parents, grandparents, older siblings or other important people.
- ◆ *Modelling* Where the child is shown the script drama through seeing others in the family living it, for example through game playing: 'Actions speak louder than words.'

2 Verbally:

- ◆ *Attribution* Attributing qualities to the child and then treating the child as if these attributions are true (transaction). For example, 'He's the intelligent one' (attribution) followed by 'You'll know the answer to this!' (transaction); 'She's a tomboy' (attribution) followed by 'You live to climb trees' (transaction).
- ◆ *Explicit instruction* For example, 'Think of others before yourself.'

Key script choices

These are the main themes of the script that link to the client's contract and must be worked with to meet the contract. There will be other aspects of the script that, for the purposes of the contract, may be ignored.

Case example: Angela
Key script choices

Angela's story has three key script aspects, which relate to her feelings of worth:

1 *Sacrifice* Putting her own wants and needs second to those of others, and making herself unimportant.
2 *Pleasing others* Behaving in ways that are pleasing to keep her family around to give her strokes.
3 *Being strong* The drive to be strong backs up the drive to please by helping her to cut off from what she feels and get on with what has to be done, providing for others' wants and needs.

The script matrix

A number of matrices have been devised to map script.[9] They have the advantage of allowing you to see the script in pictorial form, giving a snapshot of the main features. A client's script matrix is a useful reference tool when planning the work, allowing you to check that you have taken account of the key features and that nothing significant has been overlooked. A modified version of Steiner's matrix is one of the most straightforward to use; it is shown in Figure 4.2. The different forms of message are as follows.

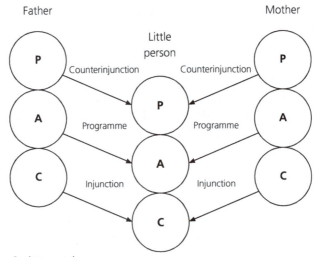

Figure 4.2 Script matrix

Adapted from the script matrix in 'Script and Counterscript' by Claude Steiner, originally published in the *Transactional Analysis Bulletin*, Volume 5, Number 18, pp. 133–5, 1966. Reprinted here with permission, Claude Steiner and the International Transactional Analysis Association.

The *counterinjunction* is a strong message from the Parent ego state of the actual parent (or significant other) to the Parent ego state of the young person. This message fits the social and cultural context in which the family live. It is given verbally and retained at the forefront of memory as an instruction about how to live life and achieve goals. Five categories of such messages, known as 'drivers',[10] have been identified:

◆ Be strong.

◆ Be perfect.

◆ Please me/others.

◆ Hurry up.

◆ Try hard.

These messages drive us into script behaviours.

◆ Which are your predominant drivers?

◆ How do they affect your work with clients?

The second form of message is the *programme*. This is a message about how to follow the script and is delivered from the contaminated Adult of the parent (or significant other), thereby contaminating the Adult of the developing young person. This message will be both verbal and non-verbal, and gives information which supports the script. For example, in a script that requires hard work and denial of personal needs, the parents might tell the young person to work hard with little or no time for fun and relaxation. These script behaviours will also be modelled to the young person by the parent.

The third type of message is the *injunction*. Injunctions are powerful messages, usually delivered non-verbally from the Child ego state of the parents (or significant other) to the Child ego state of the young person. They are transmitted from the first day of life and may even begin in the womb. What is transmitted here are the unresolved conflicts of the parents. Twelve major categories of such messages have been identified:[11]

◆ Don't exist.

◆ Don't be you.

◆ Don't (do anything).

◆ Don't be a child.

- Don't grow up.

- Don't be well (healthy).

- Don't think.

- Don't feel.

- Don't be close.

- Don't belong.

- Don't be important.

- Don't succeed.

Often we are unaware of our injunctions, following them automatically and without thought, at great cost to ourselves.

- Which are you most aware of in yourself?

- What permissions can you give yourself as an antidote?

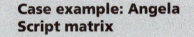

Case example: Angela
Script matrix

Angela's script matrix is shown in Figure 4.3.
    The *counterinjunctions* delivered by her mother are:

- Please others (in order to be wanted and to do good in the world).
- Try hard (to meet the goals we set).
- Be strong (and cut off from what you feel and want).

That from her father is:

- Please others (in order to be wanted and so the family will survive).

The *programme* is one of self-sacrifice. In recounting their own family stories to Angela, her parents described and modelled this message.
    The *injunctions* delivered by her mother are:

- Don't think about what you want, do what the family want you to do.
- Don't succeed (fail in your goals like I did).

◆ Don't grow up (stay the baby of the family).
◆ Don't have needs (deny them).

Those from her father are:

◆ Don't be important (in your own right).
◆ Don't feel your own feelings (feel for others).
◆ Don't have needs (deny them).

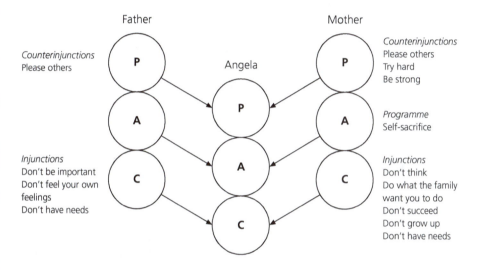

Figure 4.3 Angela's script matrix

Adapted from the script matrix in 'Script and Counterscript' by Claude Steiner, originally published in the *Transactional Analysis Bulletin*, Volume 5, Number 18, pp. 133–5, 1966. Reprinted here with permission, Claude Steiner and the International Transactional Analysis Association.

Analysis of key permissions

> True permissions are merely permits, like a fishing licence. A boy with a fishing licence is not compelled to fish. He can use it or not as he wishes, and he goes fishing when he feels like it and when circumstances allow. Permissions are the chief therapeutic instrument of the script analyst because they offer the only chance for an outsider to free the [client] . . . The Therapist gives permission to the . . . Child by saying either 'It's all right to do it', or 'You don't have to do it!' Both say to the Parent, 'Let him alone.' . . . A permission allows [the client] to be flexible, instead of responding with fixed patterns.[12]

Permissions give flexibility; they allow choice. They are positive parental influences, the gold of our psychological inheritance. For the counsellor, permissions are psychological strengths to be built on and used in the service of the contract goals.

Case example: Angela
Key permissions

In terms of her contract, Angela has two key permissions:

◆ To be loved and lovable (against all odds) and to get on with others and be close to them.
◆ To be a trailblazer and do what others have not managed to do.

At the moment these permissions are linked to conditions:

◆ Being lovable and being close are linked to pleasing others.
◆ Being a trailblazer is linked to doing things others have yearned to do.

Angela has permissions that can be used with limited autonomy. This is quite a common occurrence. It will be important to help Angela separate out and relinquish the conditional basis of her permissions so that she can use them with real flexibility without recourse to family limitations. For example, Angela can only be a trailblazer if she sets her trail in the direction her family wants and on condition it does not take her away from home. She needs to set herself free from these conditions if she is to be truly autonomous. Then she can become a real trailblazer, making choices and taking risks as a mature woman.

Analysis of Angela's story

◆ *Ego image*   A tense anxious child, trying not to have wants and needs, who wants to curl up in a lap and be reassured.

◆ *Ego state structure*   See Figure 3.3.

◆ *Stroke balance*   Mainly conditional positive.

◆ *Time structuring*   Activity and pastiming are the two main structures.

◆ *Roles on the drama triangle*   Initial role is rescuer; moves to victim.

◆ *Main game*   Happy to help.

◆ *Script matrix*   See Figure 4.3.

◆ *Key permissions*   You are lovable; you can be close; you can trailblaze.

Agreeing a shared understanding of the client's situation

Specifying key features of the client's script

Once you have made an analysis of your client's script, the next step is to *specify* with the client its key features.[13] These will be referred to as counselling progresses. Agreeing key features is vital and underpins future counselling interventions.

Your approach needs to take into account the following:

◆ the client's personality

◆ preferred ways of communicating, for example, thinking, feeling or behaviour

◆ how the client psychologically protects himself against emotional pain (defence mechanism)

◆ the level of discomfort the issue being specified might raise

◆ their dominant ego state

◆ drivers.

Example

Let's take a specification in which the client is reluctant to acknowledge to himself that the breakup of his family home was not the total responsibility of his 'hard hearted' mother, but that his father, whom he idealized, played a major part.

In the following we explore different ways of specifying based on individual client needs.

Specification with a client who has a strong thinking function
When the client has a strong cognitive function, thinking through the key aspects will be most facilitative, especially if the counsellor provides their rationale.

Counsellor: Your mother's hard heartedness seems to be linked with the great amount of time she spent on her own looking after things.
Client: Yes, my father couldn't take much responsibility domestically, he was home so little.
Counsellor: I imagine that put more pressure on your mother.
Client: Yes, it must have.
Counsellor: It seems that they both had a part to play in the breakup.
Client: It does, doesn't it? I don't think I had wanted to see it like that.

Specification with a client who has a strong feeling function
When the client has a strong need to express feelings immediately, specification through facilitating felt experience is most effective.

Counsellor: You obviously feel a lot of love for your father.
Client: I adored him.
Counsellor: It can be painful to recognize flaws in those we love.
Client: I couldn't bear to.
Counsellor: All of us make errors; it's part of being human.
Client: [*weeping*] I know things were made worse by dad's being away so much.
Counsellor: It seems likely that both your parents had their part to play in the breakup.
Client: [*weeping*] I know.

Sometimes specification is *challenging* for both client and counsellor. The relationship is deepened once this hurdle has been overcome. Most clients experience relief as they assimilate previously unacknowledged truths.

Case example: Angela
Specification

The counsellor began by specifying some of the straightforward parts of Angela's script with her. Because of Angela's desire to strengthen her Adult function and her openness to considering new views, the counsellor began with a cognitive approach, initially summarizing the key features of the story. This helped Angela to contain her feelings through the strengthening of her thinking capacity. The transaction and analysis are as follows.

Counsellor: It sounds like you come from a family where putting others first has been the norm.	Putting self last.
Angela: Oh yes, mum and dad have always put themselves last.	Agrees about parents.
Counsellor: Your conception was a surprise and not welcomed at first. [*Angela nods*] But despite both their own surprise and family advice to the contrary, your parents insisted on keeping you and have always been loving with you.	Family is loving.

Angela: Nobody could have had a more loving family.	Agreed.
Counsellor: Because of the age gap between you and your siblings you have usually been treated as the 'baby' of the family, a role which, on the whole, you describe yourself as accepting.	Position as the family 'baby'.
Angela: Well, yes, I don't really like it now. I think they forget how old I am.	Makes distinction between past acceptance of role and current dislike.
Counsellor: Would you like your family to show you they see you as a grown woman now?	The counsellor asks if Angela would like to establish a new position in her family as a mature woman.
Angela: Definitely!	The first outspoken expression of autonomous desire to change scripting.

The counsellor's reflections

Angela's counsellor is slightly surprised at the strength of her feeling at this early point. It is the first time she has shown such a strong individual viewpoint. She has done it sooner than her counsellor expected. Angela is demonstrating a keen willingness to 'grow up' and to begin to establish a new identity as a mature woman in her family.

Her counsellor decided to abandon her original plan to specify all key script features of her story to date as this would undermine Angela's developing autonomy.

The counsellor made a mental note of the outstanding specifications:

◆ Angela's fear of failure, first experienced at private school and latterly over her job
◆ her fear of letting her family down, which is closely linked with her right to exist (is she wanted if she doesn't please and meet others' needs?).

The latter point will probably emerge spontaneously in following Angela's lead in working with her frustration and conflict about how to 'grow up'. The former may need to be introduced by the counsellor at another time if it does not spontaneously emerge.

The counsellor continues

Counsellor: What would you like them to do?	Exploring the issue raised.

Angela: Treat me like the others. You know, stop fussing so much. Let me make my own mistakes.	Specifying the change in the family.
Counsellor: What would your part be in this?	Exploring Angela's own role.
Angela: What do you mean?	Angela doesn't understand. This is probably a new idea.
Counsellor: I was thinking that you have a choice about whether or not to follow your own view or listen to the 'fussing'.	Shares own thinking as a 'springboard'.
Angela: I see what you mean. [*Silent pause*] Why don't I just do it?	Angela explores this new idea.
Counsellor: That's a really important question you've asked yourself.	Stroking self-exploration.
Angela: I don't know. [*pauses again*] I suppose I'm scared.	Finds her own answer to her question.
Counsellor: What are you scared of?	Inquiring about her fear.
Angela: Mum and dad being disappointed with me.	Specifies her fear of disappointing her family. This issue has indeed emerged spontaneously as predicted.
Counsellor: That's an important realization. Do you think there's any link between your feelings of anxiety and panic around work and your fear of disappointing your parents?	Stroking. Suggesting a specification that makes a link between Angela's symptoms and her fear.
Angela: I hadn't thought about it. There could be. I had been thinking of changing jobs before all this happened. I don't think they would have been happy about it.	Specification agreed. Angela reveals an important piece of information.

Angela and her counsellor go on to discuss the links and arrive at a revised therapeutic contract, Angela will find out how she scares herself into not following her autonomous choices.

Deciding what to specify

Deciding what to specify needs careful planning and should always be linked to a full TA analysis. The chief consideration is to avoid frightening the client's Child by making a specification that is too challenging or painful at this point. The counsellor has to judge from her knowledge of the client where the boundary on this lies. If the counsellor goes beyond what the client can tolerate the client will usually show discomfort. This is an important warning sign to the counsellor to stop.

Reviewing the counselling

An important landmark in the counselling relationship has now been reached. The client has told their story more fully and key features of the script have been specified. This is hard proof that the client and counsellor are able to work together effectively. The initial therapeutic contract now needs review to ensure it is grounded in an understanding of script. At this time both client and counsellor should be given the opportunity to comment on their view of the progress to date. It is an opportune moment to invite the client to give feedback to you by commenting on what she has found helpful and what has not been useful. This allows you to adjust your approach and tailor it more closely to the client's needs. This openness of feedback helps to further build a secure and trusting relationship based on equality and respect.

Summary

We have explored the deepening of the therapeutic relationship as the counsellor and client face the challenges in confronting psychological games and the key features of the script. The client is much more aware of the choices she has made from script and the resulting thoughts, feelings and behaviours which limit her potential. She may now be experiencing frustration and a desire to move on and make changes in her life. This is a decisive point in the work when the contract is reviewed. In the next chapter we will see how the counselling work deepens as the counsellor begins to challenge the client's frame of reference.

Key concepts that have been considered include:

◆ psychological games

◆ drama triangle

◆ script choices

- script matrix
- permissions
- script features.

Key skills and techniques we have used are:

- game identification
- game analysis
- script analysis
- permission analysis
- specification
- challenging
- contract review.

Exercises

4.1 Select a character from television, novel or biography. Identify:
   (a) the position on the drama triangle most used by the character
   (b) the key psychological game
   (c) the key permissions used in a positive way
   (d) the key permissions used to further the script.

4.2 The character in Exercise 4.1 is your client.
   (a) Draw their script matrix.
   (b) Formulate a contract that would help the client make changes that would enhance their potential and autonomy.

4.3 (a) Identify the main way in which you limit your potential in your work with clients.
   (b) Formulate a contract that you can make with your supervisor that would help you expand your counselling skills.

Notes

1   E. Berne, *Games People Play* (Penguin, Harmondsworth, 1964/1985), p. 44.
2   S. Karpman, 'Fairy tales and script drama analysis', *Transactional Analysis Bulletin*, 7, 26 (1968).

3   '"Raising" children is primarily a matter of teaching them what games to play. Different cultures and different social classes favour different types of games': Berne, *Games People Play*, p. 151.

4   Karpman, 'Fairy tales', p. 52.

5   Berne, *Games People Play*, pp. 145–6: happy to help 'is consistently helpful with some ulterior motive. (S) he may be doing penance.'

6   Ibid. Berne's thesaurus of psychological games remains the single most useful reference source.

7   Ibid., p. 145.

8   E. Berne, *What Do You Say After You Say Hello?* (Corgi, London, 1974/1987), p. 418.

9   F. English, 'Sleepy, spunky and spooky: a revised second order structural diagram and script matrix', *Transactional Analysis Journal*, 2, 2 (1972). C. Steiner, *Scripts People Live* (Bantam, New York, 1974/1982), p. 105. S. Woollams and M. Brown, *Transactional Analysis* (Huron Valley Institute, Ann Arbor, MI, 1978), p. 177.

10 T. Khaler, 'Drivers: the key to the process of scripts', *Transactional Analysis Journal*, 5, 3, 280–4 (1975).

11 R. Goulding and M. Goulding, 'Injunctions, decisions and redecisions', *Transactional Analysis Journal*, 6, 1, 41–8 (1975).

12 Berne, *What Do You Say After You Say Hello?*, pp. 124–5.

13 'Specification is a declaration . . . categorizing certain information . . . The object is to fix certain information . . . so that it can be referred to later': E. Berne, *Principles of Group Treatment* (Grove, New York, 1966/1978), p. 234.

Further reading

The drama triangle

Karpman, S. (1968) 'Fairy tales and script drama analysis', *Transactional Analysis Bulletin*, 7 (26): 39.

Psychological games

Berne, E. (1964) *Games People Play*. Harmondsworth: Penguin.

Script

Steiner, C. (1974) *Scripts People Live*. New York: Grove.

Specification

Berne, E. (1966) *Principles of Group Treatment*. New York: Grove, Chapter 11, pp. 234–5.

Part Two

Developing Awareness

5 · Challenging the Frame of Reference

So far the counselling approach has mainly focused on helping the client to expand on their experience of their difficulties and to analyse the links with their personal history. The goal of this initial phase has been to put down the bedrock for the work – the counselling relationship – and to arrive at a shared view of the main features of the problem. The work is now entering a new phase. The client will need to examine some of their established ways of looking at themselves and their world in order to develop a fresh perspective on their situation. This is never easy. Most of us cling tenaciously to our established ways of seeing things. It is human nature to try to hold on to what is known. There is more security in the familiar than in the unknown.

As this phase begins, your main aims are to:

◆ review the contract

◆ challenge the client's frame of reference

◆ develop insight and awareness.

You will need to:

◆ find an effective way of helping the client to question their view of themselves

◆ agree what is to be challenged and what is off limits

◆ agree acceptable and unacceptable ways of challenging

◆ renew and develop the contract

◆ enable the client to become aware of their internal dialogue and its source

◆ strengthen the client's thinking so that they become an ally in the counselling.

Preparing the therapeutic ground

Decontamination of the Adult: the client's frame of reference

In TA this stage of the work is known as decontamination.[1] This process is aimed at strengthening the boundaries around the three ego states, thus removing any Parent or Child contaminations of the Adult. A contamination is when the boundary of the Adult ego state is 'invaded' by the content of the Parent or Child ego state (Figure 5.1).

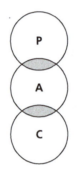

Figure 5.1 Contamination

Reprinted with permission from Souvenir Press Ltd. Eric Berne (1961) *Transactional Analysis in Psychotherapy*. London: Souvenir Press

In the process of growing up the child's capacity to think for itself and define reality is undermined by parents, significant adults and the culture. These influences put pressure on the developing child to experience reality according to their frame of reference.

Example

His mother is giving some instructions to eight-year-old Joe about how he should spend his time. The reality is that mother has a headache and Joe, full of energy, is making a lot of noise playing football against the garage wall. Instead of telling Joe the truth she redefines the situation, confusing him into suppressing his desire to play.

Mother: Go and visit your Uncle Bob, he gets lonely these days.
Joe: I don't want to, I'm having fun.
Mother: You can play when you've done your duty and been kind to poor Uncle Bob.

Joe: I don't want to go, he's miserable.

Mother: He's not miserable. You're just a selfish, lazy boy. Do as I say or I'll put your football in the bin! [*threatens*]

[*Joe reluctantly agrees. Mother strokes him to support the decision to put Uncle Bob's needs first and play later.*]

Mother: You're such a good boy. Always make sure you put other people before yourself and you won't go wrong in life.

Constantly under this kind of pressure, Joe grows up unable to play without feeling guilty (Child contamination of the Adult) and believing that he should make sure that everyone and everything is taken care of (Parent contamination of the Adult) before he can have time for himself. Consequently in adult life Joe is unable to relax and becomes increasingly stressed, finally presenting to his GP with tension headaches.

Decontamination work is achieved in four main stages:

1 *exploration* and expansion of the problem

2 *identifying* internal messages about how to live our life and relate to others

3 *challenging* unhelpful internal messages that drive the person to live in ways which cause distress and anxiety

4 *mobilizing* the client to use their Adult to think through new options on how to live and be.

This process strengthens the working alliance between counsellor and client. During this phase the client will need to become aware of their established view of their life, themselves and other people: this is known as their *frame of reference*.[2] The frame of reference:

◆ is the unique way in which the individual sees the world

◆ controls the way we perceive and understand

◆ screens out, or redefines, anything that does not fit the frame

◆ strongly influences our feelings, thoughts and actions

◆ holds the script intact.

To confront our belief system and recognize blind spots is challenging. It generates anxiety and fear. Our frame of reference is built up from before birth. Initially, it exists in the hopes, dreams, aspirations and fears of our parents and the way they project these onto us. As we develop we actively take on some of these qualities together with the particular frame of reference of our family and culture. Creating a frame of reference is an appropriate and necessary part of the socialization process. It helps ensure survival, predictability and well-being for us in our family as well as in the wider social milieu.

A frame of reference is developed therefore to suit particular social and psychological circumstances. For example, Nick's father was aggressive and violent. Nick developed a frame of reference that prized personal control because this gave him the greatest safety. During our lifetime our frame of reference may need adjusting to meet changed circumstances. For Nick the need to be so strongly in control had an alienating effect in intimate relationships. Learning to share control became crucial in establishing satisfying relationships.

Challenging

In this second phase of the work, decontamination, the counsellor will usually make *intentional challenges* to the frame of reference. This may alter the nature of the established therapeutic bond with the shift from a mainly empathic stance to one that is both empathic and challenging. Relationships of all kinds go through this change, whether they are mother and child, lovers, or counsellor and client. A sharing of difference follows the honeymoon period. Toddlers want the opportunity to go off and explore and enjoy their emerging individuality. Mothers need time out to regain their separateness. Lovers have tiffs and start to look at how they are different. This raises questions which lead to dialogue and new understanding, deepening the relationship.

The strength as well as the weakness of the counselling alliance is that only one of the partners, the client, faces consistent personal challenge. This creates heightened vulnerability for the client and a skewed distribution of power between the client and the counsellor. The client is required to deepen their trust and the counsellor to tread with ever increasing prudence and wisdom, as a guest in another's inner world.

Supervision gains importance. The counsellor submits their work to scrutiny by an independent professional and must themselves be open to challenge. Supervision provides a safety net for both the client and the counsellor by monitoring that the correct approach is being used and interventions are effective.

Key skills

The main skills the counsellor will need to focus on:

◆ empathic attunement: paying exquisite attention to the client's non-verbal and verbal responses in order to detect discomfort or feelings of shame
◆ incisive thinking: to identify links between here-and-now experience and childhood experiences
◆ clear feedback: to assist the client to hear and integrate the feedback from Adult
◆ congruency: honest reflection to the client based on observation.

How to challenge

Let's now look at what is meant by 'challenging'. The intention of challenge is to create a questioning attitude so that established ideas, feelings and behaviours are opened up to review. With most clients an oppositional or confrontational stance is at best unhelpful and at worst harmful, leading to either a polarization of positions or compliance in the face of counsellor dominance.

Non-verbal challenging

A questioning attitude can be facilitated in many ways: for example, by not responding in an expected way to a comment and leaving the echo of the client's statement to ring in the space between you (crossing the transaction with silence).

Example

A male client is talking about his difficulty in finding a girlfriend.

Client: I always make an idiot of myself with the girls I most like, ha! ha!

The counsellor makes no verbal response, but looks at the client in a warm and inquiring way. The client stops laughing, gradually falling silent. An expression of sadness crosses his face. The counsellor's non-verbal challenge has questioned his use of self-deprecating humour ('gallows humour'[3]) and helped the client notice how he ignores his pain.

Client: The real truth is I'm bloody lonely and most of the time I'm too scared to admit it.

Challenging by using a Nurturing Parent ego state

Using a Nurturing Parent ego state to indicate that something may not be in the person's best interest is another helpful way of challenging.

Example

Here the client is discussing ways to improve her health.

Client: I'm tired of feeling unhealthy. I'm going to give up cigarettes, chocolates and alcohol and start an intensive programme of exercise.

Counsellor: That sounds like a very big change of lifestyle. Our bodies usually respond better to gradual changes. Have you considered a more gentle approach?

Client: How do you mean?

Counsellor: Well giving up cigarettes, chocolates and alcohol at the same time is a tall order in itself. It can often take quite a while to adjust.

Client: I know. I did it once about five years ago. But I got so bad tempered my husband begged me to go back to them.

Counsellor: How do you think an intensive exercise programme would be on top?

Client: Probably impossible! [*pause*] But I've got to do something. I can't go on like this. I feel like I'm letting the kids down . . . setting them a bad example. What else can I do? [*becoming tearful*]

Counsellor: I can hear how desperate you feel about this. What about making a more gentle start and gradually cutting down whilst slowly building up your exercise routine?

Client: I'm afraid I won't get there.

Counsellor: Which way do you think gives you the best chance of reaching your goal?

Client: Well if you put it like that. Yeah! I didn't keep to it the hard way before did I? And I do want to do it this time.

Challenging using humour

The use of humour can be very effective with some clients in creating a non-threatening but potent challenge.

Example

The client is very angry with her boss.

Client: I'm never speaking to him again!

Counsellor: Not speaking to your boss could cause some interesting communication problems for you!

Client: [*laugh of insight*] That's true! I suppose I'll have to find another way to let him know how badly I feel treated.
Counsellor: Didn't you say your annual appraisal was due soon?
Client: Yes.
Counsellor: Would that be a good time?
Client: Well, yes, it would, wouldn't it?

Choosing specific ways to challenge

Before we challenge we do need to plan the most suitable way to do this with the client. Empathic attunement, observation and incisive thinking will best help us to analyse which method of challenge suits the client.

How do we know a challenge has worked?

The essence of challenging is to bring clients face-to-face with inconsistencies, for example between what they say and what they do, or between what they think and what they actually feel. But how do we know when a challenge is effective ? There are two main ways in which the client signals this:[4]

◆ a moment of silence will follow the challenge (*reflection*); and/or

◆ the client will give a laugh or make a facial expression of insight (*illumination*).

Extra-sensitive clients

Some clients are especially sensitive and perceive criticism in the mildest of challenges, and sometimes even when no challenge was intended. Their self-esteem is tissue thin (even though they may appear robust). They need constant unconditional positive stroking; conditional negatives puncture their confidence. It is usually quite easy to spot people who are in this group because unintentional errors generally occur early on, especially through not giving a rich enough supply of unconditional positives. Characteristically, such failures lead the client to react with strong disappointment or strong anger. The counsellor usually feels reprimanded and carries mild anxiety about making such an error again. These clients are best left to come to their own view of their circumstances without the use of intentional challenge. They will usually do this if consistent empathy and unconditional stroking are used. A process of self-inquiry and the use of bull's-eye transactions are generally the best way of helping them accomplish this.

Example

The client is in a conflict. His elderly father is very near the end of his life. On the one hand he might continue for several weeks but on the other he could die at any time. Earlier in the year the client booked a very expensive holiday, which he is now due to take. The pressure of the conflict about whether or not he should go is showing in feelings of irritability.

Client: He never did anything for me when I was a child. I don't see why I should hang around and give up my holiday just in case he dies. He never thought of me!

Counsellor: It's a very difficult dilemma for you. You feel wronged by your father, and yet you feel this could be your last goodbye. It's a big decision. [*The counsellor is empathic and uses a bull's-eye transaction.*]

Client: He's got me in the corner again. Even when he's dying he keeps his grip.

Counsellor: What's that corner like?

The counsellor feels tempted to point out that the client, in the here-and-now, can now make his own choice; his father has not put him in a corner. A direct challenge to the client's frame of reference would give the counsellor immediate relief from her own desire to become judgemental. The counsellor wisely avoids this and instead takes a more empathic approach, beginning a process of inquiry into the client's feeling of being cornered. Encouraging expression of this held feeling would release some of the painful conflict from earlier times and make it easier for the client to come to a decision in the here-and-now.

Moving to a challenging style

With the exception of those clients who are exquisitely sensitive to challenge, the first step in preparing the ground is to discuss the nature of this new phase of work with the client. The harmonizing intention of the existing empathic approach needs to be linked with the intention to make foreground the particular aspects of the client's life which are contributing to their present difficulties and which will be questioned or challenged. Bearing in mind the following points will facilitate this transition:

1 Specification (described in Chapter 3) has made a bridge for this shift in approach and should have provided ample information about what style of challenge the client is likely to prefer and what they find unhelpful.

2 The shift in approach must be gentle and sensitive within the existing relational norms.

3 Be the person you've always been for the client. Don't become a different person through changing style too much. Otherwise the client will feel they have lost you and therapeutic rupture will occur.

4 Check out what the client is experiencing following the challenge.

Checking consent to challenge: contract review

In challenging the frame of reference the counsellor is in effect holding up selected aspects of the client's experience for their inspection. The counsellor must give clear *explanations* and ensure the client has ample opportunity to ask questions, clarify their understanding, and discuss any concerns. This discussion forms part of a *contract review*, required by the change in the counselling approach, in which the client's informed consent is checked out. The discussion needs to be grounded in fact.

What aspects of the frame of reference do you, the counsellor, want to put on the agenda? It is essential to give a reasonable overview of the main areas whilst also pointing out that as the work proceeds new issues may need to be considered, or anticipated ones may turn out to have little relevance and no longer be focal.

- The counsellor needs permission to alter the itinerary according to what emerges, but always with the best interests of the client in mind.
- The client needs to decide if they give their consent to this.

Example

The counsellor begins the initial discussion about moving toward an approach that will question the frame of reference. First the counsellor explains the plan:

Counsellor: When we began working together you saw your main goal as becoming more assertive.

Client: Yes, that's right.

Counsellor: How far do you feel you have come with this goal?

Client: Well, I've got a lot more understanding of the problem but I still get really stuck in being nice. I don't seem to be able to stop myself.

Counsellor: That was my impression, too. You are probably ready to take the next step and question some of your internal beliefs that keep you in that old pattern.

Client: Mmm.

Counsellor: Your Child and Parent will need more opportunity to express their very different thoughts and feelings. Your Parent wants to keep you polite and childlike and your Child is scared to step out of line.

Client: I know. How can I do that?

Counsellor: Both Parent and Child need to be given a voice so that you can decide in the here-and-now how you want to be and move out of the conflict.

The client agrees to the plan but wants more information. The counsellor offers a general description of the approach, initially by replying to the client's earlier question:

Counsellor: There are a number of ways. One useful one is to speak aloud the comments both Parent and Child make inside your thinking.
Client: That sounds a bit embarrassing.
Counsellor: It can feel that way initially. I can suggest some techniques that would help you. Generally most people find they soon get used to it.
Client: I might not be one of them!
Counsellor: Well that's always a possibility. If you don't like how we are working, you can say so and we will stop and find a new way. Would you say 'no' if you needed to?
Client: I'm not sure.
Counsellor: Do you think you might just carry on to please me?
Client: I might.
Counsellor: Is there anything I can do to help you tell me how you're finding the approach?
[*The counsellor recognizes that the contract will require the client to do the very thing she is finding difficult, to be assertive, and so offers to help.*]
Client: I don't know. [*The client reflects for a few moments.*] It would help if you asked how I'm finding it.
Counsellor: That's good idea! [*Stroking the client for being assertive.*] When should I do it? [*Encouraging further assertion.*]
Client: A couple of times a session.
Counsellor: OK – that's a deal!
Client: I'm really shocked at myself. I've just told you what I want haven't I?
Counsellor: You have, yes.
Client: I'm already doing it. I can't believe it.
Counsellor: You can believe yourself – you did it.

The contract has been reviewed and agreed. The counsellor will now need to go on and discuss how any new related issues that may come up will be incorporated into the work, so that a way for making changes is agreed.

Keeping the client in power

As a way of redressing some of the power differential it is important to discuss the client's 'dos and 'don'ts', what is permissible and what is off limits. This gives the client control too. One of the main dangers with therapeutic confrontation is that the client will feel exposed, humiliated and shamed by the process because something they had been unaware of is highlighted as a glaringly obvious aspect of their difficulty. This can occur even with the most sensitive of approaches. By giving the client a real say in things, any potential shaming is lessened and the client is aware that the counsellor has a genuine desire to avoid it. It is also a good idea to agree an *emergency cord*, a signal the client can use if they are experiencing counsellor error or an unpleasant reaction to an intervention. An emergency cord needs to be something the client would definitely do, even when experiencing their worst-case scenario. It needs to be simple, easy to do, and tried and tested. It may be a single word such as 'stop!' or 'wait!' Or it may be non-verbal, a hand gesture, a movement such as standing up, or the use of a tool such as a specially placed small handbell. The importance of paying attention to such matters cannot be overemphasized.

Failure to prepare the ground with the client can be the single cause of failure of an otherwise excellent intervention. Remember to:

◆ agree the boundaries of what can be challenged

◆ identify the emergency cord

◆ stay attuned and respond to potential signals of shame

Case example: Tom

It had taken Tom some time to feel relaxed with his counsellor. He was still inclined to pull back and blame himself for anything he said that needed clarification or led to a minor misunderstanding. His most frequent comment at such times was, 'I'm sorry. It's my fault. I'm not very good at this.' Obviously any challenge would have to be very subtle and framed in the most sensitive of ways with Tom firmly in charge, otherwise he would be likely to use the counselling to further his conflicting script need to be perfect on the one hand, but always feel like a failure on the other.

Tom's parents had been killed in a car crash when he was 10 years old. An elderly maiden aunt whose financial assets far outweighed her capacity for human warmth and love became his legal guardian. She disliked children. Tom was sent to boarding school. There a kindly house master recognized the isolation of the shy, bereaved boy and did all he could to be a father figure to young Tom. Tom felt reassured. But returning to his aunt during holidays generally caused him to plummet into mild depression from which he only emerged when he returned to school. When he was 17 he was summoned to the headmaster's office where he learned his aunt had died from a heart attack. Tom felt numb. His aunt's solicitor became trustee of his now considerable wealth. Having no particular idea of what he wanted to do, Tom entered university and then joined a merchant bank. Although Tom was good looking, he was shy and unconfident. This prevented him finding a girlfriend. By 35 he had dated innumerable women but never been able to establish a lasting relationship. He was lonely and depressed and saw his life going nowhere.

Tom had made a good superficial bond with his counsellor. He was punctual, kept all his appointments, and talked about his loneliness. But there was something missing. It was as if he were going through the motions of talking about himself without actually being present. His counsellor felt as if she was trying to talk long distance on a badly connected telephone; communication was faint and halting. She was having a first-hand experience of what went wrong in his close relationships and why they failed to deepen. This continued over several sessions and caused feelings of powerlessness and helplessness as she consistently tried and failed to reach the real Tom, the part of himself he had walled off. She felt as if she were failing him, that he wasn't thriving with her. Discussing this in supervision she realized that her experience paralleled Tom's: she was feeling his despair whilst Tom himself kept his feelings behind his wall. Tom would have to be prepared to open up a little and let some of his feelings out. As she pondered how to put this to him, she became increasingly conscious of his vulnerability. She felt like a new mother holding a babe in her arms.

After considerable reflection the counsellor decided to challenge Tom's frame of reference through using a metaphor he himself had introduced earlier, that of a wall. This would help minimize any possibility of Tom's feeling criticized or exposed. Transactions would ostensibly be Adult–Adult; Tom's Child would be spoken about in the third person. This would protect his Child by lessening the intensity of focus on it.

Counsellor: We have done a lot of really good work together, Tom. It seems to me that the next step is for me to find a way to help you make an opening in your wall so that more of shy Tom can peep out and let us both know what he feels. How does that sound to you?

Tom: It sounds OK, but shy Tom wouldn't want to do more than peep.

Counsellor: That was my thinking, too. He doesn't want to feel exposed or put on the spot. He needs us to be very sensitive. Where in his wall would Tom feel OK about making a small opening?

Tom: We could take out a couple of bricks near the bottom. Then shy Tom won't feel his wall is under threat and he will be able to peep out without anyone being able to see in.

Counsellor: Good idea. What you and shy Tom need to know is that this will make a big difference. Even though it's only a couple of bricks.

Tom: What kind of difference will it make?

Counsellor: Well I can't say exactly. But there'll be a two-way link between shy Tom and the world after years of that link being blocked off. I imagine it might feel a bit scary at first.

Tom: I think it might. [*There is a long silence as Tom stares reflectively into space.*] I think it will be OK. [*pause*] Yes. [*long pause*] Yes.

The counsellor went on to discuss with Tom his 'dos' and 'don'ts'. For him it was most important to know that if he wanted to stop, his counsellor would respect this and not urge him to go any further. He had no particular 'dos'. As an 'emergency cord' it was agreed that Tom would use a comment he made when running meetings at work: 'Thank you, we'll stop there for the moment.' Although quite a long statement, it was one he was accustomed to using and came as second nature to him; there was no doubt in his mind that he would make use of it if he felt the need.

Summary of decontamination work

In the first part of this chapter we have focused on moving into the second phase of the counselling work, decontamination. We have enabled the client:

◆ To challenge his frame of reference, which is keeping him stuck in old patterns of relating to himself, other people and the way he views his life and problems.

◆ To strengthen his Adult. He is beginning to make links for himself between his script (outdated ways of thinking, feeling and behaving developed through childhood experience) and his difficulties in the here-and-now.

Through interventions aimed at keeping the client in power we are now able to utilize the client's strengthened Adult as an ally in the counselling. In a way he has become a co-therapist. We can now move on to making more direct interventions, which involve the client in becoming more active in steering the work. This next phase will mobilize the client to externalize the internal dialogue and to begin to experiment with new ways of thinking, feeling and acting.

Revisiting the internal felt experience

Ego state dialogue

This technique can be carried out in a number of ways.[5] The counsellor invites the client to separate out his three ego states, Parent, Adult and Child; to imagine they are sitting on different chairs; and to move between the chairs, creating a dialogue between the ego states. The Parent and Child speaking to one another usually dominate the dialogue and the counsellor invites the client to periodically move into the Adult position to summarize and intervene.

Ego state dialogue is a very helpful method for separating out the thoughts, feelings and behaviours of the different ego states and exploring these from within the client's internal experience. Most of us are so familiar with our internal dialogues that we don't recognize how they can lead us away from our real wants and needs. The people who have influenced the creation of our frame of reference now inhabit our brain and determine the way we think about others, the world and ourselves. We experience this as internal dialogue.

Externalizing ego state dialogue has two main functions:

◆ a *clarifying* function enabling us to hear which influences have stayed with us and continue to effect us

◆ a *distancing* function, allowing us to stand back and listen in to what we are saying, creating the effect of overhearing ourselves.

Powerful realizations or *insights* result. The impact of overhearing our self is the same as the impact of overhearing someone else speak about us. It makes us stop, think and question.

Setting up an ego state dialogue

Typically, three chairs are used, one to represent each ego state, with the intention of externalizing the dialogue between Parent and Child which normally only occurs internally. The Adult ego state takes on the role of mediating between the two and determining reality. Normally this function is lost or diminished by the strength of the Parent–Child dialogue, which tends to take over. Ego state dialogue helps strengthen Adult functioning. At the end of a piece of ego state dialogue, clients are often intrigued by what they have heard themselves say. Internal comments that they have taken for granted as 'reality' wither and lose their power in the cold light of day.

How to create the ego state dialogue

First of all, describe the technique to the client. Invite them to set up the three chairs, and to say how each one represents an ego state. It is more useful for the client to do this as they might choose different types of chair to represent the experienced qualities of an ego state: for example, a tall stiff chair to represent a stern Parent ego state, and a low stool to represent a fearful Child ego state. Also the space between the different chairs will carry meaning. However, if we simply have access to plain chairs then this will not affect the process. The Adult is usually placed between Parent and Child to highlight its mediation function.

Tell the client they are free to move between chairs as they speak from different ego states.

The client then chooses a starting chair, usually either Child or Parent, depending on which side of the dialogue feels most powerful at that moment. They talk out loud the words, from the chosen ego state, that usually are only heard inside their own internal world. When the client has finished speaking from one ego state they move chairs to speak from the other. The dialogue is directed at the empty chair representing the ego state that has just 'spoken'. This continues until:

♦ resolution is agreed; or

♦ one ego state gives way; or

♦ an impasse occurs.

An *impasse* is a 'no-go' or stuck position, where both ego states hold fast to their position. When it is reached, if it cannot be resolved straight away, it should be specified (to restate what the client has said in order to clarify the impasse), with an agreement that it will be revisited in the following session.

During the dialogue, the Adult must always be brought in by inviting the client to move into the Adult chair. In practice, this is often at the suggestion of the counsellor, because the client is often caught up in the Parent–Child dialogue. The Adult will play an important role in helping reach resolution or in highlighting that an impasse has been reached. At the end of a piece of ego state dialogue, ask the client to move to the Adult chair and give a summary of the work.

Sometimes clients feel embarrassed about talking to chairs and consider it exposing and unhelpful. If a client doesn't want to use ego state dialogue it is important to respect this. Any technique is only useful if the person using it is comfortable with it. The technique may need modifying to suit the client (or the practice setting). A helpful modification might be to ask the client to speak the different parts of the dialogue in turn from the one seat – 'What does your Child say?' 'Do you have a Parent response to that?' 'Does your Adult agree?' – and so on. Some clients feel more comfortable with this kind of modified technique.

Dialoguing with the Child and the Parent

Once the technique has been agreed, the next step is to decide which ego states will take part in the dialogue. We encourage the client to examine and explore the content of Parent and Child ego states in order to be more specific and to identify which Parent influence they want to speak with and which Child ego state they want to give expression to.

Parent ego state

The Parent ego state is not simply a conglomeration of all the parental influences on our development. Rather, it consists of the major figures that dominate unique aspects of our experience and tell us how to think, feel and behave in specific situations. Some are benign, but others are toxic and destructive to autonomy. The more someone has influenced us in the past, the more that person will dominate and direct our Parent ego state in the here-and-now. It is useful to break down the content of the Parent by separating out the individual people who inhabit our Parent ego state. This enables us to identify the influence that each particular one has. It is helpful to remember that the person who we listen to in our heads is usually delivering the instructions from their own Parent or Child ego state. Thus messages are often passed down from generation to generation. Using ego state dialogue, the client can then speak directly from and to figures from the past.

Child ego state

This is not one single Child ego state. Rather it consists of many separate Child ego states, each representing a different developmental phase. Berne defined these as 'a set of feelings, attitudes and behaviour patterns which are relics of the individual's own childhood'.[6] Usually known as the 'inner child', we have separate 'states' which often can be easily identified. For example, 'the baby', 'the 2-year-old', 'the teenager' are many ways in which we describe each other or ourselves. Each of these different ego states will have its own distinct and unique set of feelings, attitudes and behaviour patterns related to the epoch in which it developed.

The Child experience can be explored in detail, identifying early experiences of the individual. As the client further explores each ego state he will deepen his understanding and will begin to experience a greater ability to decide which ego state he wants to relate from, and is likely to show more self-containment of Parent and Child impulses.

Case example: Tom

Tom's internal dialogue was clearly between a cold, harsh, punishing Parent ego state taken on from his aunt, and a Child ego state who felt deeply unloved and had been forced to retreat as the only line of defence left to him. Tom preferred to use only one chair. He began from Child.

Child: I feel really lonely. Nobody likes me.
Counsellor: How come you feel nobody likes you?
Child: I don't know. [*pause*] There must be something wrong with me.
Counsellor: What could be wrong with you?
Child: I shouldn't be here.
Counsellor: You shouldn't be here.
Child: No.
Counsellor: How come?
Child: I don't know.

The counsellor decides Tom's Child has probably come to an initial stopping point and that it will probably be useful to bring in the Parent (Tom's aunt). She will check this with Tom.

Counsellor: I think it might be a good idea to hear what your aunt has to say. What do you think?
Child: I don't know. [*pause*] I'm scared.
Counsellor: What are you scared of?
Child: She doesn't like me.
Counsellor: Well that is frightening. How about we see what your Adult has to say about this?

The counsellor deliberately uses 'we' to signal to the scared Child that he is not alone. She suggests the Adult comes in to support the Child, whilst she stays alongside. This is to help Tom strengthen his ability to tolerate and soothe his own scare. If she attempts to do it directly herself, she is taking away from Tom the opportunity to learn how to mediate his problematic feelings. This could promote unhelpful dependency.

Child: Well – yes, that seems all right.
Counsellor: Tom's Adult, do you have anything you can say about bringing in the Parent?
    [*The counsellor puts it this way in order to give Tom time to change ego states: shifting always requires a few moments.*]
Adult: Yes, I do. [*talking to Child*] Tom this is important for you, and you're not on your own this time. I think you should try it.
    [*Tom shifts back to Child.*]

Child: OK.

Counsellor: So Tom's aunt, what would you like to say?

   [*Again the counsellor gives Tom time to shift ego states.*]

Parent: I'm not happy about this. All this emotion is unnecessary.

Counsellor: Say some more.

Parent: You have to get on with life. Too many people spend too much time feeling sorry for themselves.

Counsellor: Are you talking about Tom?

Parent: Yes. He's got everything to be grateful for. He's well off, got a good job.

Counsellor: He's lonely.

Parent: Pah! Lonely. That's self-indulgence. You're better off on your own. You can't trust people. They just want your money.

Counsellor: That's a strong statement.

Parent: Well it's true!

Counsellor: Tom wants to find someone to settle down with.

Parent: He's better off on his own.

Counsellor: What makes you so sure?

Parent: I've seen people hurt. You're better off without other people interfering.

Counsellor: Have you been hurt?

Parent: That's none of your business.

Counsellor: I'm sorry, I didn't mean to be offensive. I just sensed someone might have hurt you.

Parent: Well, I might have been. But I don't want to talk about it.

Counsellor: No, of course not. Thank you for telling me.

The counsellor recognizes the huge admission made by the Parent. It isn't necessary to go any further at this point, and the Parent has clearly indicated this is a stopping point. There is now enough of a chink in the Parent's armour to give the Child room to feel more self-assured. The Child needs an opportunity to share what it has made of the Parent's admission.

Counsellor: Tom's Child, did you hear that? [*Again, giving Tom time to shift ego states.*]

Child: Yes. I didn't realize that's how things were. It changes the picture doesn't it?

Counsellor: It does.

Child: It's not all me is it?

Counsellor: No, no, it isn't.

Child: It's hard to take in after all this time. [*pause, then as if speaking to himself*] It really isn't me.

Tom sits reflectively in silence for several moments, obviously assimilating what he has heard. When he looks as if he is ready to talk again, the counsellor speaks.

Counsellor: Do you feel ready to talk?

Child: Yes.

Counsellor: How about we ask your Adult their view?

Child: Yes. OK.

> [*It is important that Tom integrates the experience of both ego states in Adult to complete this piece of work.*]

Counsellor: Tom's Adult, will you tell us your views?

> [*There is a slight pause and Tom shifts almost imperceptibly on his chair.*]

Adult: Well I think it's clear, isn't it, why the Child feels like it isn't wanted. The mystery is cleared up. The Parent doesn't trust people and doesn't want them around. It's got nothing to do with Tom himself.

Counsellor: That's right.

Adult: Tom doesn't need to feel bad anymore. This isn't about him.

Counsellor: You're right.

Tom has taken a big step in confronting his belief that he is unlovable and his feelings of not being good enough. Together with his counsellor he has challenged his frame of reference. Tom has now 'taken out a couple of bricks' from his wall and is beginning to let his counsellor glimpse his Child. Through this process he can now see that the real problem lies with someone else (his aunt). The difference between Child experience, Parent introject and Adult reality has become crystal clear.

In the next sessions Tom will need to really understand what this means for him and the way he leads his life. More work will need to be done on how he continues to make sense of it and the impact his new awareness will have on his life. In the next chapter we will look at how he does this with his counsellor.

Key skills

As the counsellor moves into this phase she will need to develop her creativity and intuition, 'sensing' which Parent or Child ego state might be dominant at any given time and responding with sensitivity and directness. Many counsellors in training begin to express some fear or anxiety as they begin to work with challenge- and technique-based work. They need the support of their supervisor as they develop the courage to challenge and experiment. Don't be afraid to be afraid! Letting ourselves know what we feel as we develop our counselling skills and expand our repertoire is all part of the learning process. As you try out the exercises at the end of this chapter, focus on what you are experiencing as you role play.

Summary

In this chapter we have discussed the importance of identifying and challenging the client's frame of reference as well as how to challenge different clients and recognize if the challenge has been accepted. We then explored how to move on to working directly with the client's internal dialogue that keeps the frame of reference alive. The methods discussed are aimed at:

◆ deepening the client's insight

◆ challenging the frame of reference

◆ keeping the client in power

◆ giving voice to the inner Child

◆ hearing the Parent

◆ strengthening the Adult.

In the next chapter we will look at how to build on this work in order to complete the changes our client is making in this phase.

Key concepts used in this chapter are:

◆ frame of reference

◆ contaminations

◆ decontamination

◆ impasse.

Key skills include:

◆ explanation

◆ contract review

◆ observation

◆ analysis

◆ ego state dialogue

◆ challenging

◆ empathic attunement.

In the next chapter we develop the work, expanding further the client's awareness of their internal dialogue and enabling them to take charge of it.

Exercises

5.1 (a) Select a client and decide their frame of reference.

    (b) Draw their contaminations.

    (c) Decide what would be the most helpful way to challenge this client and why.

    (d) Find a partner to play the client and role play the unhelpful way of challenging. Discuss why this approach isn't helpful.

    (e) With your partner as client, role play the helpful way of challenging. Discuss why this approach is facilitative.

5.2 (a) With your partner, set up an ego state dialogue using three chairs. Each of you should take a turn to be 'the client'.

    (b) After the dialogue is complete, discuss your experience of using this method: (i) as a client (ii) as a counsellor.

    (c) Identify your learning goals, both internal and external, and what you will do to realize them.

Notes

1   E. Berne, *Transactional Analysis in Psychotherapy* (Souvenir, London, 1961/1980), Chapter 4, pp. 47–50: 'Insight in the process of psychotherapy comes about when the Adult is decontaminated and the proper boundary between the Child [Parent] and Adult is re-established.'

2   J. Schiff and A. Schiff, 'Frames of Reference', *Transactional Analysis Journal*, 5 (1975), pp. 290–4.

3   E. Berne, *What Do You Say After You Say Hello?* (Corgi, London, 1974/1987), Chapter 17, pp. 337: 'The gallows laugh or the gallows smile occurs after a special kind of stimulus and response called the "gallows transaction". A typical example is an alcoholic who has not had a drink for six months, as everyone in the group knows. Then one day he comes in and lets the others talk for a while. When they have gotten all their troubles off their chests, so that he has the stage to himself, he says: "Guess what happened over the weekend?" One look at this smiling face and they know. They get ready to smile, too.'

4   'The insightful laugh . . . marks a therapeutic success', p. 235; 'Parental laughter is indulgent or derisive. The Child laugh in the clinical situation is irreverent or triumphant. The Adult laugh, which is therapeutic, is the laugh of insight', p. 288; E. Berne, *Principles of Group Treatment* (Grove, New York, 1966).

5   Some of the well-known approaches to ego state dialogue include: E. Stuntz, 'Multiple chair technique', *Transactional Analysis Journal*, 3 (1973), pp. 105–8; J. McNeel, 'The Parent interview', *Transactional Analysis Journal*, 6 (1976), pp. 61–8.
6   Berne, *Transactional Analysis*, p. 69.

Further reading

Frame of reference

Schiff, J.E. (1975) *Cathexis Reader: Transactional Analysis Treatment of Psychosis*. London: Harper & Row, Chapter 5, pp. 49–71.

Decontamination

Berne, E. (1961/1980) *Transactional Analysis in Psychotherapy*. London: Souvenir, Chapter 4, pp. 47–50.

6 · Freeing the Adult

As we saw in the last chapter, a crucial milestone is reached when the client is able to recognize the difference between their Child or Parent ego state and their Adult. But this is only the beginning of awareness. The force of the internal dialogue between Child and Parent may still very easily take over, when the client is under stress, and create temporary loss of Adult awareness by contaminating it. To free the Adult from this intrusion, further work is needed.

Your goals are to:

◆ expand awareness

◆ assess client change.

What do you want to achieve? On completion of this phase there will be a number of outcomes. You will enable your client to:

◆ take charge of their internal dialogue

◆ build a more positive stroke balance

◆ take charge of their transactions

◆ reduce psychological game playing

◆ finally, decide together whether to complete or continue the counselling.

Expanding awareness

The internal dialogue

A useful way to think about the therapeutic work ahead is in terms of psychological energy. Child and Parent are highly charged with the energy of both past experiences and the views of others. Once the client has Adult awareness, their Adult becomes free from Parent–Child contaminating influences and is able to hold back or keep *bound* the *force* of the energy, pushing it back and containing it, in the ego states from which it originates.[1] In stressful situations the Adult will find it difficult to resist this pressure and may be overpowered by the force of energy of the Parent and Child, especially once their internal dialogue kicks in. At such moments the energy becomes *unbound* and floods Adult awareness.[2] Often a seesaw effect occurs at this phase of the work. Bound energy becomes unbound and floods Adult awareness, and must then be rebound again (often only with the help of the counsellor in the early stages), allowing the Adult to function freely and without interruption. Clients often feel frustrated and disheartened by this movement of energy within their psyche, which, to the client, seems to happen of its own volition without any warning and against their desires. Like learning any new skill, there are setbacks before skilled mastery is attained.

What can the counsellor do to help? The best approach is consistent analysis of the times when the unbound energy has flooded the client's Adult and overwhelmed it. This usually means regularly discussing and analysing the times between sessions when the client has experienced a loss of Adult awareness, and helping the client to identify the triggers that cause this to happen. In this way awareness is continuously expanded and strengthened. Clients need clear *explanations* of this process, particularly why it occurs. They also need to know that it is *normal* and will eventually stop.

Case example: Tom

A few weeks after his realization that his aunt's view of him was inaccurate and biased by her own experience, Tom arrived at his session in a depressed mood. Encouraged by his growing confidence in himself he had invited a woman from his office out to a restaurant for dinner. They had had a pleasant evening and things seemed to have gone well. A few days later Tom had phoned her to suggest another evening out. She hadn't accepted. In Tom's words, 'She didn't exactly say "no", she just didn't say "yes".' Tom had taken the rebuff to heart and plummeted into feelings of self-loathing, self-criticism and despair. The full force of his Parent–Child dialogue took over. Because he had been relatively free of it for a few weeks, the impact was especially powerful. His tolerance for his negative feelings about himself had imperceptibly decreased without him realizing it. He hadn't appreciated how much better he was beginning to feel about himself. The contrast felt too much for him. To have tasted freedom and then suddenly to be thrown back into his prison had destroyed his budding hope and strengthened his despair. He said that he couldn't see any point in going on with counselling. He obviously didn't have what it took to benefit from it. He apologized for being difficult and wasting time and asked if the counsellor would accept two weeks' fees in lieu of notice. He was sorry to have let her down.

The impact of Tom's despair was searing. Two small tears formed in his counsellor's eyes. She gave him a look of great warmth.

Counsellor: Tom, I can see how desperate you're feeling, but this is normal. Most of us feel this way when we start to go against our script messages. Most people feel like giving up at some point on this part of the journey.

Tom: You've been very kind and I am very grateful for all you've tried to do. You don't have to let me down lightly. I'm sorry to have failed you.

Counsellor: Tom! You aren't listening to me; you're listening to the words in your head. I'm telling you the truth. This is normal. It's a temporary hurdle. I know you're feeling overwhelmed by disappointment but . . . [*Tom interrupts*]

Tom: You don't understand. I can't bear the pain; it's too much for me. [*He starts to cry.*]

Tom cries quietly for a few moments. His counsellor indicates her presence by making soothing sounds. This is the first time he has cried. It is a milestone. The impact of the rejection has punctured his bound Child ego state and caused his pain to flood out. As his tears subside his counsellor begins talking to him.

Counsellor: There are years of pain that you've had to lock away because nobody would listen. It's different now. You and I can talk about this. You're not on your own with your pain.

Tom: I don't know if I can stand it.

Counsellor: It won't always feel like this. As you get more used to the yeses and the nos of closeness it will become easier. The first time is always the worst.

Tom: Do you really think I can do this?

Counsellor: Yes, I do.

[*Tom is silent for a few moments.*]

Tom: I don't know why you believe in me. But it seems to make a difference. I'll give it a go.

Counsellor: I'm really glad. Shall we take a look at what happened and how you felt about it?

Tom: Yes.

They go on to look at how Tom's Parent launched into extreme criticism of him when his invitation wasn't accepted. His confidence collapsed under the attack and his Child felt more despairing than ever. As Tom analysed the sequence of events and linked it to his internal dialogue, his Adult became empowered and he was able to put the rebuff into a more realistic perspective, recognizing that on his quest to find a partner he would probably receive several rejections and that it would be important to separate them from the magnitude of his childhood rejections.

Because he was vulnerable to his internal dialogue at this time of change, his counsellor offered him an additional session. Tom also agreed to contact her by phone if he began to feel overwhelmed.

What happened?

The rejection that Tom experienced when he tried to arrange a second date with the woman from his office acted as a powerful trigger, unbinding his Child energy and reawakening past feelings of being unwanted and unloved. The unexpectedness of his colleague's refusal took him off guard and added power to its impact on his Child. His Child energy overflowed, flooding his Adult. His Child distress gave the hitherto bound and quiescent Parent an opportunity to seize back its former power from the Adult. The Parent started up its tirade of critical denigration with renewed vigour after its period of relegation by the Adult. It, too, flooded the Adult with its own unbound energy. Tom felt at the mercy of the combined energies of his Parent and Child, which seemed to have drowned out his Adult. He became desperate and despairing. Having put his faith in counselling, he had felt encouraged when he realized he was really starting to feel better. He had dared to hope. As his progress had continued his hope had grown. Fear of relapsing into his previous state of mind lessened. He was beginning to forget how he used to feel and had lowered some of his defences. Because of this, the impact of the rejection was heightened and had in fact penetrated to a layer of wounding that had lain buried since childhood. Tom truly felt worse than he had for many years. His script messages restarted with a vengeance:

◆ I'm not lovable, nobody wants me (Child, injunctions: you're not lovable, you can't get close).

◆ You're bad because you can't get it right (Parent, driver: be perfect – I knew you couldn't!).

By the time he arrived at his counselling session he was convinced he was beyond the help of his counsellor.

Why didn't Tom's counsellor warn him?

Tom's counsellor knew that Tom's internal dialogue was still alive and that Tom had begun a process of gradually strengthening his Adult. There would be times when his Adult would be overwhelmed by the joint power of Child and Parent. She had discussed this with Tom in an earlier session and prepared him as much as was possible for what he might experience. In fact there was no way of knowing the specific nature of what he would experience. When the first time came Tom forgot the discussion with his counsellor because of the overwhelming pain of his feelings. Nothing can be done to prevent circumstances like this occurring. It isn't possible to predict what clients will meet as they journey beyond their scripted pathway. This is one of the reasons why a good therapeutic relationship is essential. It is often the key factor in holding a client through turbulent times.

On the positive side, such experiences can be worked with to prevent them being script reinforcing by helping to release emotions locked away since childhood and to build awareness.

What did Tom's counsellor do?

The first thing Tom's counsellor did was to *normalize* his experience. She reminded him that although shocking in its impact, his experience was not unusual, that most people undertaking personal change go through a time of feeling back in the grip of their scripted internal dialogue which leads to the temporary reassertion of their frame of reference. Normalizing is a crucial intervention in times of distress. It helps to cut through hopelessness by providing reassurance that the person is not having an abnormal experience. Normalizing provides a useful lever with which to help the client push back and begin the process of rebinding Child and Parent so that the Adult can emerge uncontaminated.

Tom doesn't show a direct response to the normalizing. In fact he appears to be disregarding it because he cross-transacts from Child, cutting across his counsellor. She has been talking overtly to his Adult, but certainly wanting his Child to overhear by using what is known as an *angular transaction*. An angular transaction is transaction from Adult, which addresses both the *social level* (in this example Adult to Adult fact) and the *psychological level* (reassuring the Child) (see Figure 6.1).

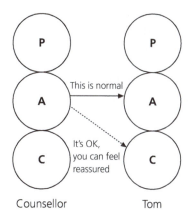

Figure 6.1 Angular transaction

Reprinted with permission from Souvenir Press Ltd. Eric Berne (1961) *Transactional Analysis in Psychotherapy.* London: Souvenir Press

Tom's response comes straight from Child (hitherto he has been in contaminated Adult: I'm not a suitable client, I'll leave), showing that his Child has indeed heard but is not reassured. He moves fully into Child and reveals his pain in its pure rawness. Although he is not reassured, the fact that he is willing to trust the counsellor with his pain and despair, and *to cry for the first time*, is an indication of the continuing durability of his alliance with her. The relationship continues to be strong.

Key skills

Tom's counsellor accepts and contains his grief with nurturing warmth. Like comforting a child needing solace, she is soothing, reassuring and patient, waiting until Tom is ready to talk. She goes on to offer him an *explanation* of his predicament and a new approach to working with it.[3] She makes herself uncompromisingly focal with Tom, *modelling in the present* that others do want closeness with him and do find him lovable and valuable, showing him that, in fact, his frame of reference with its prescribed script roles of isolation and rejection is false. Once again, Tom seeks reassurance; he needs to know his counsellor believes in his ability to be close to others. He is borrowing some of her hope. Eventually, Tom feels sufficiently reassured and decides to carry on.

As Tom discusses the circumstances of the rejection, his counsellor helps him to separate out the past and the present. She helps him do some reality testing about the process of finding a partner, helping him to reassert what he already knows but forgets in moments of distress – that some rejection is par for the course. This will strengthen Tom's Adult and build awareness.

Finally, Tom's counsellor offers her vulnerable client important *protection*:[4] she arranges another appointment later that week and telephone contact as needed. These protections are to counteract any sense of abandonment, to give Tom access to help if he needs it, and to enable him to strengthen his Adult. It is always essential to increase protection when a client is vulnerable so that maximum support is given to their emotional self.

The necessary key skills include:

◆ soothe and reassure
◆ patience
◆ explanation – counsellor may teach aspects of TA theory to strengthen insight
◆ modelling in the counselling relationship
◆ reality testing – separate past from present
◆ offer protection by increasing support.

The external dialogue

Our internal dialogue strongly influences our transactions or external dialogue. We behave in ways that fit with our internal perceptions of ourselves, others and the world. Our transactions are a direct reflection of our inner world. As the client grows competent and skilled in recognizing and understanding the difference between Child, Parent, contaminated Adult and genuine Adult, they will need to develop increased awareness of their interactions with others and whether these are script reinforcing (non-Adult) or *autonomous* and Adult.[5]

Case example: Tom

Several weeks after his failed attempt to date his colleague, Tom was becoming self-assured once again. When he lost Adult awareness he was generally able to recognize it and rebind the Child–Parent dialogue. Immediately following the crisis, he had met with his counsellor on a twice-weekly basis. This increased frequency of contact had given him a feeling of security whilst he re-established his self-confidence. After two weeks he had reverted to his usual weekly frequency.

Tom had three more attempts at finding a girlfriend. Each time the same thing happened. The first date went well but nothing followed. A clear pattern was emerging, which puzzled and upset Tom. He couldn't understand what happened. His counsellor suggested they see if common factors could be found that would give some clue about the problem.

Tom always made the first approach. The woman always seemed surprised and slightly taken aback. This pleased Tom because he felt he was making a powerful impression and definitely not coming across as someone who couldn't get a girlfriend. At this stage he felt good about himself and believed the woman was impressed with him. It seemed to take very little persuasion to move to agreeing a date and time for a meeting. Tom felt euphoric in the days leading up to the date. On the day itself he always arranged for a posy of flowers to be delivered. He arrived at the restaurant 20 minutes early to make sure everything was in order, and by the time the woman walked in a bottle of chilled champagne was waiting at the table to be uncorked the moment she sat down. Tom would have rehearsed several topics of conversation, 'just to make sure we don't run out of things to say'. Tom felt the evenings always flowed smoothly. He never pressed anything further, drove the woman home in his sports car, giving her a light kiss on the cheek as he bade her goodnight. The following day he would send her a note thanking her for a pleasant evening. He would continue to feel very positive. After five or six days Tom would ring up to arrange another meeting. Each time he was surprised to be met with a feeling of 'coolness', which always took him off guard. He knew immediately that a second date was out of the question. He would come off the phone and plunge into that familiar feeling of despair. 'I just can't understand it. What do I do wrong?', he asked his counsellor.

How did Tom's counsellor work with him?

Positive stroking: affirmation

Tom clearly put his all into making the evening as perfect as possible. His counsellor decided to begin by giving him positive strokes for his kindness and meticulous attention to detail. She thought that he hoped to find a rich source of conditional positive strokes from the women he dated. Each time he felt stroked negatively and unconditionally. The first priority was to avoid repeating the process in the counselling and, instead, to provide Tom with some of what he both wanted and needed, positive strokes.

Counsellor: You are thoughtful and generous in the way you plan the evenings. It sounds like you do everything in your power to make the evening special.
Tom: [*flushing slightly and shifting in his seat*] Well, yes I do.

Although Tom doesn't say much it is obvious from his flush of pleasure and his bodily movements that he is pleased and feels recognized. The next step is to build his *insight* by helping him to look back over events and consider what might have contributed to the failure of his hopes. Developing hindsight is always the first step in gaining insight.[6]

Insight: hindsight

The counsellor invites the client to use hindsight to recall the problem situation and identify the key issues contributing to the psychological game.

Counsellor: With hindsight, Tom, does anything stand out as possibly contributing to the problem?
Tom: I've asked myself that question. The only thing I can think of is I might have come across as too keen.
Counsellor: [*gently nodding 'yes'*]
Tom: I mean . . . I suppose . . . well flowers and champagne on the first date might seem quite a lot to some people.

The counsellor expresses agreement, responding with gentle para-verbal and non-verbal responses to confirm her agreement and to support Tom's view in a way that she hopes will feel empathic. She wants to avoid causing him to feel any further pain, rejection or embarrassment whilst assisting him in building an accurate picture of his mistakes.

Analysis of Tom's actions

The next step is very delicate. She must facilitate his awareness of the impact, of so much contrived giving, on the women he dates. Tom needs to be able to appreciate that his behaviour may feel controlling and intrusive. He also needs to recognize that he is objectifying people by treating each woman according to the same formula. He isn't recognizing their individuality and giving from a desire to cherish their unique qualities and preferences. Tom's perfectionism and involvement with his own plans is blinding him to how he is treating his partners.

Confrontation

Tom will need to understand the discrepancy between his perceived good intentions and the reality of his behaviour. Confrontation of this discrepancy has to be made if he is to deepen his understanding of relationships.[7] It will be hard for him to accept and there is a risk that he might yet again become self-critical and despairing.

Counsellor: Did you notice any differences in the women you went out with?

Tom: How do you mean?

Counsellor: As people, in what ways were they different from one another?

Tom: It's easier to start with how they were alike.

Counsellor: How?

Tom: Well they were all tall and blonde and quite a bit younger than me. Mandy and Barbara work in personnel and Lisa works in accounts. They're all good fun.

Counsellor: Are the qualities you've mentioned the things that attracted you to each of them?

Tom: I hadn't thought of it like that, but yes, I suppose so.

Counsellor: How is Lisa different from Mandy?

Tom: She's quieter. More serious. Doesn't seem as confident.

Counsellor: So might Lisa like different things from Mandy?

Tom: Well, yes, I suppose so.

Counsellor: How do you imagine Lisa felt inside when the champagne was opened almost as soon as she sat down?

Tom: It's funny you ask that. She said she didn't usually drink. Now I come to think about it she didn't look very pleased. She seemed to get a bit tense.

Counsellor: So with hindsight you think she may not have enjoyed the champagne. Perhaps, given a choice, she may have ordered a different drink, even a non-alcoholic one.

Tom: I see what you're driving at. It's obvious. No wonder she didn't want to see me again. What an idiot I've been. [*Tom slumps in his chair and covers his face with his hands.*]

Counsellor: No Tom, you haven't been an idiot. You genuinely intended to make the start to the evening as nice as possible.

Illustration

Tom's counsellor has helped him to recognize his failure to see Lisa's difference. But he is on the brink of moving into a self-deprecatory place, rather than developing insight. She must try to prevent this by following up her confrontation with an illustration from her own experience which puts her alongside Tom as someone who doesn't always recognize individual qualities in others.[8]

Counsellor: I remember my son's seventh birthday party. All the boys in his class had held their parties at the local swimming baths. I just assumed he would want that, too. I had it all booked. One day I mentioned it and asked who he wanted to invite. I always remember the blank look he gave me. When I told him what I had done he was very upset. He wanted a day at the racing track go-carting. That taught me an important lesson.

Tom: [*Tom is reflective for a moment*] It helps to know you make mistakes like this, too.

Game and stroke analysis

The confrontation seems to have held with the help of the illustration. But this is only the beginning. Further supporting work will be needed in the sessions that follow to keep building insight and awareness. Now that Tom has some preliminary understanding of himself, the next step is to analyse his psychological game and its resulting strokes. Tom is already familiar with the concepts of the drama triangle.[9] In the next session his counsellor began to discuss it.

Counsellor: With hindsight, what position on the drama triangle do you think you were taking when you assumed that all the women you dated would enjoy champagne?

Tom: At the time I wouldn't have said I was. But . . . if I think about it now . . . rescuing maybe? But that doesn't seem quite right.

Counsellor: I can see why you say it. You look like you're being kind and helpful and looking after people. If you think about Lisa having to drink something she doesn't like . . . maybe she felt controlled by you?

Tom: Well then it sounds like persecutor. But how can it be? I wasn't being mean or horrid. I just went over the top on being nice.

Counsellor: I know it sounds odd. Yet you coerced Lisa into doing something she didn't want to do in the belief that you were being helpful. You persecuted from rescuer. Persecution doesn't necessarily arise from a desire to cause hurt. We can persecute when we insist others accept our well-intentioned actions.

Tom: Mmm. [*Tom lapses into a brief thoughtful silence.*] I hadn't thought about it like that.

Counsellor: Shall we look at what happened next? It might help make all this clearer.

Tom: OK.

Counsellor: Whilst you were arranging the flowers and champagne you felt happy with yourself and gave yourself lots of positive strokes.

Tom: Uh huh.

Counsellor: You probably imagined you would receive lots of positives from Lisa. Instead she gave you very few.

Tom: Yes, that's true.

Counsellor: Then when you try to arrange a second meeting you experience strong negative stroking when Lisa declines. You feel hurt and unappreciated and move to the victim position. You probably experience Lisa as persecuting.

Tom: That's it! That's exactly how I felt.

Counsellor: So you move from persecutor to victim.

Tom: Yes. It's like getting kicked just when you thought you were going to be really appreciated.

Counsellor: That's right! The game you set up is called 'kick me'![10]

Games

All games can be given a name. This is useful shorthand to enable the client to easily understand the dynamics of the game, the needs that drive the game and the outcome of the game. In his book *Games People Play* (1964), Eric Berne named and categorized the main games. The counsellor is offering Tom the definition of a game, 'kick me', identified by Berne, in which Tom initiates the game from a victim position and invites persecution. This will reinforce Tom's belief that he is bad and enable him to obtain negative strokes that confirm his existence.

It is often useful to ask the client what name they might give the game. For example, Lucy, describing a game which involved three people (three-cornered game), choose the name 'ping pong', saying she was the 'ball being batted about from side to side'.

Insight: foresight

Here the counsellor invites the client to develop foresight by asking him to think about forthcoming situations in which there is potential for getting into a game. The aim is to avoid the game or minimize the level of negative strokes. Tom and his counsellor continue in further sessions to look at how Tom can arrange dates in a more relaxed manner and so avoid playing 'kick me'.

As Tom contemplates giving up some of his meticulous attention to detail, he realizes that he is scared and anxious of spending time alone with women. All the gifts are a way to hide this from himself as well as from the women he dates. When Tom finally plucks up the courage to ask someone else out, his counsellor helps him to strengthen his insight by encouraging him to develop foresight by:[11]

◆ looking at the traps he might create for himself out of anxiety

◆ talking through his fears

◆ helping him to keep these in perspective.

Tom's next date goes much better. He doesn't get the same pre-date 'high' from his internal stroking, but also avoids the post-date 'low' of the negative strokes when, in fact, the woman agrees to a second date. The woman's agreement to a second evening out gives Tom the positive strokes he has yearned for from another; he isn't reliant only on internal positive strokes.

He is further changing his script and starting to build a new *stroke balance* that is increasingly positive and healthy.[12] The more positive strokes Tom can yield, both internal and external, the more this will reduce his drive into games and/or lessening his level of game playing.

Confirmation

Tom had a few more casual dates that continued to help him to build his confidence. Naturally, he also experienced setbacks from time to time. The counsellor was aware that at such moments she might need to confirm her original confrontation to strengthen and 'reinforce [Tom's] ego boundaries' further because he could still lapse into his original frame of reference and script behaviours.[13] And, indeed, such a moment soon came.

Tom had become particularly close to one woman and had begun to see that he might have a long-term future with her. Out of the blue, she was offered a job in another country. After much soul searching (because she, too, felt committed to Tom) she decided to accept the offer. Tom was distraught and in his distress became self-critical, searching compulsively within himself for what he had done 'wrong' and what he 'should have done differently'.

Counsellor: When you search your mind for the fine details of what you think went wrong, what do you experience?

Tom: I'm not sure what you mean.

Counsellor: How do you feel?

Tom: A bit better, I suppose. Like maybe I'll find the answer and it will all get better again.

Counsellor: Your description reminds me of the times when you tried to make perfect evenings out. I imagine you are trying to stop yourself feeling unhappy with your search for the perfect answer. You are sad and hurt, Tom. There is no answer. You didn't make an error. Life isn't always kind or fair.

Tom sits staring into space and then, putting his head in his hands, he gently weeps. His counsellor feels a now-familiar tenderness and reflects on her own feelings of sadness at being unable to prevent the painful times on his path to *intimacy*.[14]

Insight: midsight

Tom needed to strengthen his insight by becoming skilled at midsight – to recognize when he was moving into the old, script frame of reference as it was happening.[15] Midsight enables the client to work more independently from the counsellor, out there on his own, in stopping the furthering of games. It is the most difficult aspect of insight to develop. It requires the ability to:

- be reflective in mid-flow as our thoughts and feelings are unfolding

- recognize possible consequences before they arise

- contain the impulses from Child and Parent which drive the game

- short-circuit the game and change direction to a more positive outcome.

Tom and his counsellor decided that the best way for him was to come and talk through his reflections on new or challenging situations and that he would take the initiative in sharing how he had made sense of his own thoughts and reactions. He soon realized that he particularly enjoyed this aspect of the counselling. He liked taking the lead and the feeling of being in charge; after so many months of feeling dependent on his counsellor, it gave a boost to his confidence that neither of them had expected. He was delighted with himself. After a lifetime of feeling self-critical he could now feel self-approval that others shared. Even when he 'got it wrong', as he put it, he was no longer worried. He really understood that life is a process, a shifting kaleidoscope of changing feelings, thoughts and experiences whose constant momentum makes 'right' and 'wrong' unhelpful concepts in normal human contact.

During this phase of counselling Tom's stroke balance had changed:

◆ He had become increasingly used to positive strokes and no longer unawarely expected negative ones.

◆ He expected to be affirmed.

◆ His need to be 'kicked' diminished accordingly and he set up his 'kick me' game only rarely, and to a much milder degree.[16]

Tom eventually went out with another woman. This time the circumstances were different. She had asked him to accompany her to the theatre. The evening went well and romance blossomed. It was soon obvious that a deep commitment was building between Tom and his girlfriend.

It was now clear that Tom would soon be ready to end counselling.

Practising free awareness

Practising free awareness is a lifetime's activity. Awareness itself can cause discomfort and create dilemmas, which are difficult to resolve. Insight gives freedom from the frame of reference and from the script, but can also bring unwelcome realizations as we see ourselves and others 'in the cold light of day'.

Grieving for lost illusions

Tom had a very unpleasant realization. Because he had always been desperate for companionship he had always tried to please people ('please me' driver), going to great lengths to make people feel happy in his company and so want to be with him. A dawning realization crept over him. Like a child offering sweets in the playground, he had bribed people. He was wealthier than many of his peers and people enjoyed the 'good things of life' he offered – paying for more than his fair share of drinks, travelling in his expensive car, picking up the restaurant bill. As Tom had become happier and more secure, he didn't feel a desperate need to keep people around. He noticed he was starting to feel irritated with people who 'seem to expect me to pay all the time'. In tracing back the origins of the problem he saw what he had done. But he also had to face the realization that some of his 'friends' might value what he provided more than they valued him.

Slowly, Tom drifted away from some of his former associates and began making new friends, who hadn't been coerced by his wealth. It was very hard for Tom to face what he had done and for a while he felt disillusioned.

Some disillusionment and sense of loss is inevitable at this point in counselling, because the script has engendered an illusory perspective, which has been stripped away. Familiar ways of looking at life are changed forever and, whilst this has obvious positive aspects, it also causes discomfort. Facing key illusions is challenging. It leads us to re-evaluate the ways in which we have lived and brings into the foreground important people in life. Sometimes people we have previously seen in a negative light are seen in a new positive light and, as in Tom's case, those we have formerly seen positively may seem less so. Recasting people in either direction is problematic and painful because we have to alter their role, and what they mean to us, and so our ways of relating to them. Their positions in our world have previously been fixed and immutable; unexpectedly these change. Even when the relationships only exist in mind (for example, when someone is no longer alive, or we have lost contact with them), changing our view of that relationship causes temporary insecurity and anxiety. The client often enters a grieving process as they come to terms with the loss of illusions of, say, 'a happy childhood' or 'perfect parents'.

Assessing client change and making an ending

At the end of such powerful work it is important to review how the client has changed and to check that there are no loose ends. Tom's level of game playing has decreased; he rarely gets caught up in his old game roles (persecutor and victim), and instead spends more of his time in intimacy. He has changed his stroking pattern so that generally he seeks positive strokes that will be affirming for him.

Key skills

At this stage the counsellor needs to review all key aspects of the client's change to ensure that nothing significant has been overlooked. In addition to games (and overall time structuring) and strokes, keep the following checklist in mind when doing this:

- structural ego states, especially the strength of the Adult ego state and the extent to which it has become free from Parent and Child intrusion across its boundaries
- sufficient resolution of key script impasses
- sufficient resolution of relevant script injunctions and drivers
- an appropriate increase in autonomy (awareness, intimacy, spontaneity).

Analysis of Tom's changes

Tom is no longer driven by perfectionism (driver), although he will probably always have a tendency to seek high standards

1 His self-critical attitude (Parent introject) has lessened and he is now only mildly self-critical.

2 He has developed considerable ability to get close, which has come through decontamination of his Adult and the awareness that the voice that tells him he is 'bad' belongs to his unhappy aunt.

3 His feelings of being unlovable are connected with his painful childhood experiences, but do not represent the truth about him ('don't be close' script injunction).

4 He now has proof that he is lovable and can get close. He can remind himself that there was also a time in his life when he was loved by his parents.

Tom's frame of reference has changed. He is significantly more autonomous; he has high awareness, markedly improved ability for intimacy, and greater capacity for spontaneity, although this is probably the sphere in which he has made least change. In times of stress he is still inclined to become rigid in his attitudes.

It is clear that Tom has not fully resolved many of these areas, and that more work could be done. This is, however, unnecessary because his life is radically improved and he has accomplished what he set out to do. He has completed his contract and is very satisfied with the changes he has made. It is time to make an ending. Doing more than is needed isn't a good idea; it prolongs the work and can destabilize the client by throwing up new issues, which become unbound and destroy the equilibrium that has been achieved.

Making an ending

Endings are a very important part of counselling. What are the important things to finish in the counselling? The first step is to discuss with the clients their own readiness to end:

◆ Some clients want to end prematurely, often to protect themselves from fear of feeling the sadness of saying 'goodbye'.

◆ Others may want to cling fast and fear the loss of the counsellor.

◆ Some clients hear a discussion about ending as the counsellor wanting to reject them.

◆ Some will be comfortable talking about endings.

If a time-limited period of counselling has been agreed, it is usually relatively straightforward to raise the matter as the client is prepared from the start for the ending to come at a particular time. Where an ongoing contract has been agreed, natural finishing moments occur as pieces of counselling are completed. These are the times to review the work and the contract and to look at possible endings (or to recontract for further work).

Some clients prefer, and respond better to, a definite ending point. Others find a weaning approach more comfortable, perhaps cutting sessions to fortnightly or monthly as an interim step. If the counsellor thinks the way the client wants to end is not in their best interest, this needs to be discussed. But if what the client wants seems of benefit to them, then it is preferable to go with this. It is empowering. And, soon, the client will be going it alone. The counsellor needs to gradually relinquish her role (but not her presence) and help the separation process by supporting the client to take increasing authority and agency in the sessions.

How to make an ending in short- to medium-term work

Take at least two sessions to do this; if the work is very short term, then one will be sufficient.

A structure helps both client and counsellor. The following questions facilitate the ending process.

Links between past and present
◆ How have you ended relationships in the past?

- How do you want to end with me?
- What will we do that is new for you?

Reminiscence

- What have been the three most important milestones in our work together?
- As you look back, what have you found helpful?
- What didn't you like?
- Are there any moments that make you smile?
- How are you different from the way you were in your first session?

Focusing on now

- What will you miss?
- How do you feel about saying goodbye?

Ending ritual

Mark the ending by formulating a simple ritual based on client need. It is best if the client takes the lead here by deciding on how they want to end (see Chapter 10).

Tom's ending

Tom's situation was unusual because successful completion of his contract coincided with an important milestone – finding a partner for himself. The relationship with his new girlfriend became very strong and eventually they decided to marry. Tom had been ready to leave counselling for some time, but had wanted to stay until he felt settled with his new partner. Tom had no living relatives that he knew of and he wanted his counsellor to come to his wedding. As he put it, 'you're the nearest thing to a loving mother I've got. It wouldn't feel right if you weren't there to celebrate with me. It's the culmination of my work with you.'

Key skills

Whenever a client requests their counsellor to join in an external situation, it is important to look at the underlying motivation so as not to set up a psychological game. We must also consider ethical issues that might arise in the breaching of boundaries.

The way in which Tom expressed his desire for the counsellor to come to the wedding pulled at her heartstrings. And, of course, she would enjoy sharing Tom's happiness with him after his painful and courageous struggles.

Tom's counsellor gave careful thought to his request. Was he trying to cling on to her and put her in the middle of his marital relationship? Were his motives limited to those he described? How would his wife-to-be feel if she attended the wedding? How would she, herself, feel?

She talked it through with Tom. He was quite clear he wanted to end counselling. After the wedding he wanted monthly sessions for a while and then, he thought, to move to a final ending. He saw the monthly sessions as supporting him in his transition to married life. And he wanted the security of knowing he had somewhere to come and talk if he needed it. His fiancée felt comfortable with his counsellor coming to the wedding. Privately, Tom's counsellor thought he might, unaware, be holding on to her. Another way of viewing the situation might be that most people about to be married for the first time do this. Parents are important in helping a new marriage get off to a good start by playing a strong supporting role on the sidelines. She would be *modelling in the present* this function. She might conclude that attending Tom's wedding would be in his best interest.

However, the overriding decision was based on ethical considerations. At the point of ending some clients subtly attempt to alter the nature of their counselling relationship, crossing the boundary between the professional role and friendship: for example, 'I'd like to meet you for coffee', or 'come to my opening night'. This often creates dilemmas for the counsellor, who does not want to seem rejecting at this critical point, yet knows that she must hold the boundary. Endings need to be clear and well bounded, and this can be helped if the professional role is clearly defined in the very first session.

Tom needed to know that all future counselling would be based on his current relationship with the counsellor and not altered or compromised in any way by external influences impinging on the relationship. Therefore the counsellor decided to gently refuse the invitation whilst explaining her reasons for doing so.

Key skills

Supervision is very supportive when faced with these dilemmas. It is useful to explore our own emotional reactions to these types of situations or invitations from clients before deciding on what action to take. When we feel caught in a possible ethical dilemma, it is important to give space for reflection. Tell the client you need time to think the situation through and then discuss in supervision before coming to a decision.

The counsellor became aware that she was caught up in trying to deny there was going to be an ending. She had become emotionally attached to Tom and was finding it hard to let him go. For Tom to feel his disappointment and come to terms with the fact that he had no parents or loving relatives to share in his special day meant that he finally faced and worked through his deep grief.

Supervision pointers

Select a client with whom you are working and with whom you would like to use some of the skills and techniques in order to *develop awareness*.

Self-supervision

Decide what makes the client suitable for this approach:

◆ What indicates the counselling has reached a stage where the approach would be suitable?

◆ What constitutes the client's frame of reference?

◆ What will be a helpful way to make a shift from an empathy-only approach to one that is both empathic and confrontational?

◆ What will be a helpful way of introducing the client to ego state dialogue?

Supervision with your supervisor

Discuss your thinking with your supervisor.

◆ Notice where your supervisor agrees with your views and where they hold a different view.

◆ Where are your views similar to your supervisor's?

◆ Where your supervisor holds different views, what do you learn?

◆ Contract with your supervisor about how you will build on strengths and how you will develop those areas where you need to develop your learning.

Summary

Your client has made important changes which are concrete and durable. This is time for satisfaction in what you have achieved. Even when your client decides to continue (Chapter 7) it is important to allow yourself time to reflect on a job well done.

Key concepts in this chapter are:

♦ unbound energy

♦ bound energy

♦ injunctions

♦ drivers

♦ awareness

♦ insight (hindsight, midsight, foresight)

♦ time structuring

♦ strokes

♦ games

♦ endings.

Key skills we have used include:

♦ normalizing

♦ explanation

♦ protection

♦ autonomy

♦ confrontation, illustration, confirmation

♦ stroking

♦ modelling in the present

♦ angular transaction

♦ game analysis

♦ stroke analysis.

Exercises

Carry out the following exercises with a partner, using the information from the client you selected for Exercise 4.1. At the end of each exercise, explore your emotional responses to the use of the specific counselling skills outlined in this chapter, and to the client's feelings and behaviours. Also, identify the role on the drama triangle that you feel compelled to take in response to client cues.

6.1 (a) Your partner role plays your client bringing a situation where their unbound Child and Parent energies have unexpectedly flooded their Adult. Practise using normalizing and explanation to work with the issue. Discuss the strengths and areas to further develop your approach.

(b) Your partner continues in the role play. Practise modelling in the present the relationship that is needed and provide any appropriate additional protection. Discuss your strengths and areas for development.

6.2 (a) Your partner develops the role so that you can practise the confrontation–illustration sequence. Discuss your approach.

(b) Your partner extends the role so that you can practise confirmation. Discuss the work.

6.3 (a) Your partner continues in role. Analyse the client's game and stroke patterns to further strengthen insight and help lessen game playing. Discuss strengths and areas for development.

(b) Your partner expands the role so that you help the client come to terms with unpleasant realizations and support them in making appropriate autonomous changes. Discuss strengths and areas for development.

Notes

1   E. Berne, *Transactional Analysis in Psychotherapy* (Souvenir, London, 1961/1980), p. 40: 'Bound . . . [energy] then corresponds to potential energy.'
2   E. Berne, *Transactional Analysis in Psychotherapy*, p. 40: 'Unbound . . . [energy corresponds] to kinetic energy.'
3   E. Berne, *Principles of Group Treatment* (Grove, New York, 1966), p. 236: 'Explanation is an attempt on the part of the therapist to strengthen . . . decontaminate, or reorient the . . . Adult.'

4   E. Berne, *What Do You Say After You Say Hello?* (Corgi, London, 1974/1987), p. 374: 'the "three P's" of therapy which determine the therapist's effectiveness are – potency, permission and protection . . . the . . . Child must believe he is potent enough to offer protection from the Parental wrath.'

5   E. Berne, *Games People Play* (Penguin, Harmondsworth, 1964/1985), p. 158: 'The attainment of autonomy is manifested by the release or recovery of three capacities: awareness, spontaneity and intimacy . . . Awareness means the capacity to see a coffeepot and hear the birds sing in one's own way, and not the way one was taught . . . most members of the human race have lost the capacity to be painters, poets or musicians, and are not left the option of seeing and hearing directly even if they can afford to; they must get it secondhand . . . Awareness requires living in the here and now, and not in the elsewhere, the past or future.'

6   Hindsight: I have been unable to find a reference for this concept, which is not my own. My recollection is that I came across the idea in conversation with a colleague.

7   E. Berne, *Principles of Group Treatment* (Grove, New York, 1966), p. 235: 'In confrontation the therapist uses information previously elicited . . . in order to disconcert the patient's Parent, Child, or contaminated Adult . . . the therapeutic object is always to cathect the uncontaminated segment of the . . . Adult.'

8   Ibid., p. 237: 'An illustration is an anecdote, simile, or comparison that follows a successful confrontation for the purposes of reinforcing the confrontation and softening its possible undesirable effects . . . Illustration is . . . an attempt by the therapist to interpose something between the . . . Adult and . . . other ego states in order to stabilize [the] Adult and make it more difficult . . . to slide into Parent or Child.'

9   S. Karpman, 'Fairy tales and script drama analysis', *Transactional Analysis Bulletin*, 7, 26: 39–43 (1968).

10   E. Berne, *Games People Play*, (Penguin Harmondsworth, 1964/1985) p. 73: 'This game is played by men whose social manner is equivalent to wearing a sign that reads "Please Don't Kick Me". The temptation is almost irresistible . . . Then he [asks] . . . "Why does this always happen to me?"'

11   Foresight: I have been unable to find a reference for this concept, which is not my own. My recollection is that I came across the idea in conversation with a colleague.

12   C. Steiner, *Scripts People Live* (Bantam, New York, 1974/1982), p. 135.

13   E. Berne, *Principles of Group Treatment* (Grove, New York, 1966), p. 240: 'The . . . Child has only abandoned his inconsistency with some reluctance and will try to salvage at least part of it in some covert way. The alert therapist will see what is happening and will meet the Child's new mobilization with a new confrontation.'

14   E. Berne, *Games People Play* (Penguin Harmondsworth, 1964/1985), p. 160: 'Intimacy means the spontaneous, game-free candidness of an aware person, the liberation of the eidetically perceptive, uncorrupted Child in all its naiveté living in the here and now.'

15   Midsight: I have been unable to find a reference for this concept, which is not my own. My recollection is that I came across the idea in conversation with a colleague.

132 · Developing Awareness

16   C. Steiner and C. Kerr (eds), *Beyond Games and Scripts. Eric Berne, Selections from his Major Writings* (Ballantine, New York, 1976), p. 86: '(a) A First-Degree Game is one which is socially acceptable in the agent's circle. (b) A Second-Degree Game is one from which no permanent, irremediable damage arises, but which the players would rather conceal from the public. (c) A Third-Degree Game is one which is played for keeps, and which ends in the surgery, the courtroom or the morgue.'

Further reading

Explanation, confrontation, illustration and confirmation

Berne, E. (1966) *Principles of Group Treatment*. New York: Grove. pp. 235–41.

Games

Steiner, C. and Kerr, C. (eds) (1976) *Beyond Games and Scripts. Eric Berne, Selections from his Major Writings*. New York: Ballantine. Chapter 7 'Games' and Chapter 9 'Games: an Update'.

Intimacy, love, and classifying relationships

Berne, E. (1970/1981) *Sex in Human Loving*. Harmondsworth: Penguin. pp. 125–34.

Part Three

Recapturing Spontaneity and Intimacy

7 · Discovering Internal Confusion

The counselling work is entering a new phase. The client and counsellor will be working at greater depth as they go more deeply into the experience of both the Parent and the Child. The clarity of awareness gained in the previous phase of the work is the foundation upon which this next stage will build.

In this phase your main goals with your client are to:

- clarify confusion in the Parent
- clarify confusion in the Child
- consolidate the Adult position.

At the completion of the work the key outcomes will be that your client:

- can separate Parent ego state experiences from Adult ones
- can separate Child ego state experiences from Adult ones
- has integrated Adult awareness
- has changed and updated their self-concept.

Preparing the therapeutic ground

Recontracting: implications of the work

As the counselling moves into this new phase, the counsellor's first task is to discuss with the client the implications for them of this shift in emphasis. What does it mean to recapture spontaneity?

Spontaneity is the non-adapted expression of true feelings, thoughts and actions from an integrated Adult ego state. When we are spontaneous we allow ourselves to be natural. We are free and uninhibited. We don't worry about what others will think, but neither are we trying to go against them. Because we don't feel self-conscious, we aren't focused on how we are coming across to other people. We are behaving naturally, without pretence.

A common difficulty at this stage

A common difficulty at this stage is for clients to confuse genuine spontaneity with the plastic variety. When this confusion occurs it is important to tread gently and help your client to see the difference between authentic and false spontaneity. One of the most difficult situations for the counsellor to correct is when fake spontaneity is used as a licence for wilful rebelliousness. In such circumstances, the client often claims a sort of childish moral high ground with those around her, indulging unreasonable, thoughtless or irresponsible behaviour on the pretext that I am 'being free' or 'being myself'.

Example

Matthew gave the impression of always feeling rather browbeaten, first by his apparently dominant mother and later by his wife, whom he subtly blamed for his feeling of being 'second rate'. Gradually, Matthew began to change from his usual resentfully conscientious self into someone who behaved increasingly inappropriately. He began arriving late for work, he was rude to his boss, and he came close to sexually harassing one of the young secretaries in his office. Matthew justified his behaviour on the grounds that at long last he was being himself. This blinded him to the obvious possible consequences of his behaviour – that he could lose his job. His counsellor had to tread carefully. Anything that he perceived as an attempt to 'dominate' him would only increase Matthew's determination to continue on in the same way. Gradually, she was able to help him see that he was in fact acting out his angry feelings by his behaviour. He was not being genuinely spontaneous, but hitting out at the world for the years of 'domination' he felt he had suffered.

The client will be exploring and experiencing their internal world in an increasingly immediate way, recalling and re-experiencing both key qualities of their relationships with parent figures and some of their own early experiences. The aim of the counselling is *deconfusion of the Child ego state* by helping your client to make sense of their feelings and experiences. This depth of personal recall will cause energy held and previously bound in both Parent and Child ego states to become unbound. It can have a temporary destabilizing effect; your client may again feel awash with forgotten and unexpected emotions.

In the earlier phases of work the energy that was deliberately unbound by the counselling process was generally accessible to language, so that the client could name and identify both their experience and its origins with some degree of accuracy and certainty. At this stage what is being unbound is generally not easily put into words. Unbound energy and experiences are often from the preverbal stage or from the first seven years of life prior to the stage of cognitive development. Experiences are felt in the body as well as emotionally, and people often struggle to identify a clear focus or find the language to explain what they are experiencing. Typically, clients will describe strongly felt experiences which seem to have vague origins and which do not appear to fit into an easily recognized part of earlier life experience. It is as if the origins and identity of these feelings hide in the shadows. People feel dogged by the strong presence of these powerful and confusing influences. Your client may become understandably frustrated by the irresistible force of her emotions, feeling both unable to take hold of them and bring them fully into focus and equally unable to banish them. Your client may need to borrow hope, encouragement and reassurance from you that the way she is feeling is only transient. You can help by reminding your client of the wider picture, including the changes she has made already and some of the 'stuck' points successfully worked through.

Of course, it is not only your client who may feel some confusion and disillusionment. As counsellors we often feel echoes of these same feelings ourselves because of the difficulty of making clear links for the client. We can feel just as much in the dark as our client. What is important is to remain calm and centred, allowing the client's experience to emerge in its own time.

Key skills

Soothe the client. This is best done through:

◆ providing constancy, being predictable, staying steadfast
◆ demonstrating your ability to contain both your own and your client's anxiety
◆ soothing the client with non-verbal communication through an open and calm posture, gesture and facial expression and verbally with a calm steady voice and gentle soothing sounds when the client is distressed.

Reassure the client by giving clear information about the stages of counselling and what this particular stage means. For example, you might say:

TA counselling has five main stages:

1 Telling your story and building our relationship.
2 Developing insight and awareness so that you know and understand the nature and origins of your problems.
3 The working-through stage, which is the one we are in now, means that you will bring to the surface buried emotions and associated memories. This might provoke feelings of anxiety and insecurity and the question, 'Who am I?'

4 When you have expressed your held emotions and let go of past hurt, you will move on to the redecision stage. You will begin to let go of script roles as you make new choices and decisions about how you want to live your life. I will be a source of support to you as you practise new ways of being in the world.

5 Finally, when you have achieved your goals you will be ready to make an ending with me.

Some people want the enhanced freedom from script which the work will yield, whilst others do not find it necessary or even desirable. Some clients move on to this next stage whilst others decide not to do so. In moving into work that will recapture spontaneity it is very important to make a clear assessment of the client's internal resources and what they want from the next phase of counselling. To undertake this phase of work your client needs:

1 a strong Adult

2 a reasonable degree of understanding about what they are undertaking

3 a willingness to make the journey.

Goals and focus of the work

As always, recontracting is a vital first step in proceeding with the work, agreeing with the client their goals and focus. Contracts at this stage are often necessarily more implicit than explicit because of the difficulty of framing experience in concrete verbal terms. 'I want to feel less anxious', 'I want to feel better about myself', 'I want to make a better quality of life', are typical contracts at this stage of counselling. With contracts like this the counsellor will explore with the client what they mean by their statement and how they foresee the change. Trying to be too specific from the outset is unhelpful because the therapeutic thrust of the work involves the client changing their internal perceptions of key parent figures and of their own earlier life experiences. What is important is that the contract is framed in the positive, for example, 'I want to feel better about myself' becomes 'I will develop self-confidence.'

A major outcome of this phase of the work is a new internal relationship to self which, in very broad terms, results in clients liking themselves better and accepting themselves more easily. Clients feel more 'at home' with who they are. Internal relationships with key parent figures are also radically changed as the client gains the confidence to let go of introjects and see themselves and their life in new ways.

Case example: Angela

Angela had made several important realizations in the four months she had been working with her counsellor. In particular she had recognized:

◆ her desire to please
◆ her fear of really growing up and not going along with her family's wishes
◆ the extent to which she felt trapped by a vague but ever present sense of guilt and
non-entitlement.

With these new realizations and awareness of their links with her position in the family as
the 'eternal child', her feelings of anxiety and panic had disappeared. When her symptoms had abated, Angela discussed with her counsellor the possibility of ending. In many
ways this would have been fine. The difficulties (panic and anxiety) which Angela had
brought had been resolved. However, several important issues were still up in the air:

◆ What should she do about her job?
◆ Did she want to accept or change her role in her family?
◆ Was it inevitable that she was dogged by guilt?

Angela felt that without resolving some of these questions she would live in a shadow,
with a nagging doubt that her symptoms might return, perhaps in a more aggravated
form. Her counsellor agreed that this was a real possibility. Lively, determined and courageous, Angela felt strong motivation to explore these issues. She made a contract with
her counsellor to 'find out where my family ends and I begin'.

Angela's contract is loose enough to allow for the creative unfolding of her experience.
She can evolve and grow with the new discoveries she will make, supported by a contract
that points the way to her final destination but does not prescribe the pathway.

Deconfuse the Child ego state

Preparing the client for the Parent's story

Confusion in the Child ego state stems from an inner relationship with internalized parent figures that fails to support or corroborate the person's genuine
qualities. When the client attempts to self-actualize through free expression they
hear an inner voice or they experience strong physical sensations which halt their
free thoughts, words and actions. As we have seen in earlier chapters, often what
is internalized is detrimental to autonomy and made up of truths which belong

with the experience of the parent figure, not the client themselves. They are the internalized feelings, thoughts and behaviours of the other person, not Adult reality. What is internalized is an interpreted experience which may, in fact, not carry a basis in reality. For example, when Pauline was seven years old her mother became chronically ill. The pain of her illness made her irritable and short tempered. Pauline thought she was the cause of her mother's irritability because she did not understand the link between physical pain and interpersonal response. Counsellors must always remember that they are working with internal truths, not externally verifiable ones.

Deconfusing the Child ego state involves separating out the internally perceived realities of the Parent and Child from Adult here-and-now reality, so that the Parent realities do not dominate or infiltrate but are kept contained in the Parent ego state. Much of this separating out will have taken place in the earlier phase of work (see Chapter 2), but some may still remain to be done. For example, if the client had reached an impasse in an earlier phase this might only be resolved through deconfusion work.

Once the separation between Parent, Child and Adult is complete we move on to resolve the problems in the Parent. Occasionally Parent qualities are so toxic that they are unlikely to be available for resolution, and to try and work with them would only create more problems for the client. Where this is the case it is essential to stop at the point of separation. The energy in the Parent is contained and separated off as much as possible from the rest of the psyche.

Key skills

Containing toxic Parent energies

1 Do not give the Parent time or attention.
2 When the Parent tries to take over, help your client back into Adult by any appropriate means including:
   - cross-transaction
   - redefining transaction (changing the subject)
   - humour.
3 If none of these work, sit with the Parent until its energy begins to wane and then help your client move into an Adult ego state.
4 If possible, never end a session with toxic Parent dominant.
5 Where you cannot avoid ending with Parent dominant, make an extra session or agree to talk on the phone with your client, to facilitate and reinforce Adult. Don't leave your client at the mercy of toxic Parent introjects.

The client and counsellor need to agree which parent introjects are causing difficulty and directly affecting the client's ability to function freely. These are the ones to be worked with. Sometimes the decision will have been made earlier on in the work, but it is always helpful to recheck it.

Key skills

Deciding which introject to focus on

1 Identify recurrent introjects that are linked with your client's difficulties.
2 Identify the actual parent figure these are connected with.
3 What is the minimum that needs to be done to free your client's energy? For example:
   ◆ containing and shutting off the ego state
   ◆ bringing out the introjected attitudes more fully so that your client has greater awareness of them and will be able to recognize when they are interfering
   ◆ acknowledging there was something distressing for the Parent figure, and then helping the client to separate from any transgenerational 'fallout' they are carrying.

Protection and potency

We have already looked at the need to provide clients with protection; to this we now add therapeutic *potency*.[1] In general terms, being potent involves using your Adult in a way that is more powerful than your client's script. In this phase of counselling this means facilitating your client to an understanding that her Parental voices are not her own views but are inherited from a parent figure whose life and circumstances were different. These messages are unhelpful and out of date; they need to be replaced by the client's Adult understanding and awareness. During this process of moving from a parent dominated view of life to their own Adult one, your client is in a vulnerable transition. Internal Parental backlash is likely, as the parent struggles to maintain its position. Your job is to contain and confront these reactions, supporting the Child, and ensuring that no harm comes to either the Child or the Parent itself. Any failure to potently protect your client's Child would result in the script being even more strongly reinforced.

Confrontation should be accompanied by well-timed soothing of the Parent's feelings. This can be done by recognizing and acknowledging the circumstances which led to the parent figure's reality becoming dominant. However, it is absolutely vital that the Child does not feel betrayed or compromised by the understanding which is shown to the Parent. The Child must not feel that the counsellor's empathy for the Parent is greater than the empathy shown for her own plight. This would be to win the battle and lose the war.

Case example: Angela

Angela's parental confusion was linked with both her parents. From her mother she had introjected a feeling of indebtedness. Angela felt she owed a debt of love and compliance. She felt that to recompense her mother for all the suffering she had gone through in having a fourth child, she ought to be as much like the daughter her mother wanted as she possibly could.

With her father it was different. A sensitive child, Angela had understood the depth of her father's disappointment at the loss of his dreams to family life and domestic necessity. From him she had introjected thwarted dreams and frustrated ambition. Angela's drive to achieve in her professional life was linked to her father's failure to achieve. He wanted her to achieve things that had been out of his reach and she had taken this on, staying closely involved with her family and trying to realize their dreams. Her commitment to family life (which paralleled her father's) meant she had so far failed to develop a social life or build romantic relationships.

With both her parents the introjects were intensified by the love and nurture she had been given. Bonds of love held Angela captive, not bonds of anger or hatred. She said she 'never had anything to kick against'.

The Parent's story

The next step in the work is to enable the Parent to tell their story. Where two or more parent figures are involved, a decision must be made with the client about which one to work with first. Parent ego state phenomenology, the sense of the actual experience and identity of the parent figure, is most easily elicited when the client takes on the role of that person through a *Parent dialogue*. The client is encouraged to think, feel and respond from the inner world of the Parent ego state. It means actively encouraging the introject's full vitality, letting out what is usually only carried internally and giving it full expression so that it can be worked with, changing and transforming it as appropriate.

Setting up a Parent dialogue

This can be done in a number of ways. The traditional way is by using an 'empty' chair.

1 The client is asked to imagine that the Parent figure (in this case father) is seated on the empty chair.

2 The counsellor will then ask the client to describe father: his name, what he is wearing, hairstyle, how he holds his body, voice tone, gestures, facial expression and personal qualities. It is important that the Parent is described from a time in the past rather than the parent of today.

3 Ask the client to move over into the empty chair and to 'become' father. Help the client to take on the role by asking the following questions; this helps to reinstate the context of the past, thus enhancing memory recall. Reinstate the context by asking the Parent:

   ◆ What is your name?
   ◆ How old are you?
   ◆ Where do you live?
   ◆ Will you tell me about your life?

   To give immediacy to the work and to increase its effectiveness, invite the Parent to speak from the past in the present tense to give immediacy to the dialogue. Always call the Parent by their name.

4 Follow this with pertinent therapeutic questions about the relationship between the projected parent and the client in the past.

5 Be empathic with the Parent. Try to understand their situation within the context of their life. Once this empathic bond is established between counsellor and Parent, a shift will take place. The 'Parent' will usually soften and speak with empathy about the client.

6 When it is clear from the dialogue that the 'Parent's' messages to the client were as a result of their own struggles rather than because of 'faults' in the client, bring the Parent dialogue to an end and say goodbye.

7 Ask the client to return to their own chair.

8 Explore their experiences in response to what they have heard.

The empty chair is used to provide a focus for the emerging Parent and a boundary that delineates and separates the Parent, so that the client does not feel overwhelmed by the energies they unleash.

   The usual caveat applies as with ego state dialogue. If the client is uncomfortable using an empty chair, the techniques can be modified and the client can speak from where they sit. Because an internalized identity of another is being activated, it is particularly important to clarify the moment when the client becomes the Parent figure and to derole afterwards.

How easy is it to take on the role of another person?

Sometimes counsellors who are new to this technique worry that it will be too difficult for the client. In fact, most clients find it quite easy once they get over any initial hesitation. It is generally a great relief to externalize the thoughts and feelings that have been carried inside for so long, and once a client gets into the flow of the dialogue they usually find the work takes on a momentum of its own.

This type of work is powerful. When it has taken place in my therapy group, observers have commented that it feels as if another person has entered the room.

Case example: Angela

Angela decided to begin with her father. She felt that his influence was so dominant that she would not be able to see beyond it until she had worked it through. Angela felt comfortable using the empty chair technique.

She began by describing a mild-mannered man with a lively sense of humour who was fiercely protective of his family – a man whose whole life was dedicated to his family. As her father's presence became palpable in the room, Angela's counsellor asked her father's first name so that when Angela moved chairs, and fully immersed herself in the introject, she would have a name by which to address the Parent. He was called Ralph.

Angela's counsellor asked her to change chairs and to become Ralph.

Reinstating the context

The first stage is to ask the questions to reinstate the context of the past situation.[2] This helps the client to recall some of the general detail of the parent figure so that it is easier for them to fully connect with their inner Parent. After this preliminary work, Angela's counsellor moved on to asking more direct questions about Ralph's life.

The preliminary dialogue: building the story

Counsellor: Tell me about your life as a child. You come from a large family.

Ralph: Yes there were 10 of us. Mother worked hard looking after us all but she was always cheerful. Father was just the same. Worked down the pits. Long hours, poor pay. He was gifted, played the accordion.

Counsellor: Your family sound very hard working.

Ralph: I always tried to help out.

Counsellor: How did you meet Angela's mother?

Ralph: At a dance, love at first sight! I didn't think she'd bother with me, her being from a respectable family.

Counsellor: But she did.

Ralph: She did.

Counsellor: And you decided to marry.

Ralph: Yes. Her family weren't over the moon about it.

Counsellor: What about your family, what did they think?

Ralph: My father wasn't in favour. He thought Ruth would find the life too hard. He thought she'd regret it. Mother never said anything.

Counsellor: They relied on you a lot, you said.

Ralph: [*Ralph looks pensive and gazes reflectively into the middle distance for a few moments.*] Yes. It was hard leaving them. I felt bad . . . like I was letting them down.

Counsellor: That must have been difficult for you.

There is silence as Ralph sits pensively staring into space. When she judges the moment is right, the counsellor continues.

Counsellor: Angela tells me you are musical.

Ralph: I play the trumpet. I wanted Angela to take up the piano but she didn't like it.

Counsellor: You're obviously very proud of her.

Ralph: She's clever, takes after her mum. She's done well for herself.

Counsellor: She has done well. But so have you, Ralph.

Ralph: Me! I haven't done anything.

Counsellor: You were a considerate son and a caring father.

Ralph: I've done my best.

Counsellor: You had to let go of a lot of dreams.

Ralph: I did my best.

Counsellor: You put your family before your dreams. That's a big thing to do.

Stating Angela's position

Now that the relevant aspects of Ralph's story have been brought out in the dialogue, it is time to put Angela's position alongside her father's. This will emphasize the links between his story and her present circumstances.

Counsellor: Angela wants to do something different. I don't think even she knows what yet. But she feels you made so many sacrifices for her and your family that the least she can do is stay in a job that makes you proud and makes your sacrifices count for something.

Ralph: [*looking surprised*] I thought she liked it. It's a good job.

Counsellor: Your family has a history of self-sacrifice and, at the moment, Angela is following in that tradition.

Ralph: I don't know what to say. [*Ralph stares into the middle distance, deep in thought.*]

Counsellor: Angela is afraid of disappointing you.

Ralph: I'd get over it. [*His tone is suddenly bitter.*] I'd have to, wouldn't I? It wouldn't be the first disappointment I'd had to deal with and I don't suppose it will be the last.

The counsellor's reaction

Angela's counsellor is taken aback by the sudden intensity of Ralph's tone. There is more than mild-mannered, kindly sacrifice buried here. Putting Angela's feelings into the frame has provoked Ralph to show a different side. Unconsciously tensing herself against further angry blasts, she continues.

Ralph's rage

Counsellor: You gave up a lot.

Ralph: Of course I did. What choice was there?

[*Ralph's anger is increasing with every word he speaks.*]

Ralph: Why should she [*pointing at Angela's chair*] be any different? She's had everything, everything! And still she's not satisfied. I'd have been over the moon with half of what she's got. And she's not happy. Not happy!

[*Ralph emphasises his final comment with a bitter, threatening irony.*]

His rage is in full flow. After years of repression it has finally emerged, and with it the hidden reason for Angela's undue fear of disappointing her family. To follow her own path is to risk the full impact of this bitter rage. Ralph's mild exterior hides a more menacing reality.

Planning the work at the critical moment

At this critical juncture the counsellor has some key decisions to make. She must decide whether to:

1 Pursue the source of Ralph's anger in the hope of lancing it. This would assume that it is amenable to being lanced.
2 Push to see if Ralph will show understanding of Angela's situation.
3 Plan to wind down the Parent dialogue and rebind the energy of the ego state, sure in the knowledge that, as a result of the work, Angela will have a much clearer

understanding of what she has introjected. This in itself will diminish the power of the Parent dialogue.

The decision

The counsellor decided that it would be unwise to pursue option 1. The extent of Ralph's rage was an unknown quantity; to open it up further could be detrimental and would take time which could be spent more profitably in other ways. And there was no guarantee of a positive outcome.

For similar reasons, option 2 seemed equally unlikely to result in anything positive for Angela.

Option 3 seemed most likely to yield the best outcome.

Winding down the work and rebinding the energy

Counsellor: You have had a lot of disappointments, it is understandable that you feel angry. Over the years you have managed to hide it well. You have taken a real risk tonight in revealing the extent of your feelings.

Ralph: [*acknowledges the counsellor's stroke with a grunt*]

Counsellor: I hope you feel that I have understood your position.

Ralph: [*nods 'yes'*]

Counsellor: Is there anything more you would like to say before we finish?

Ralph: It wasn't easy for me, you know. It wasn't easy.

Counsellor: I can see that, I can see how hard it was for you. You had to face tough choices. There was no easy path. In many ways the best you could do was to make choices that would minimize pain and difficulty. And in doing that you lost out. Your ambitions were thwarted. And I suppose it must be difficult to know where, reasonably, you can direct your anger. After all, no one is really to blame. Circumstances were against you. You have kept your anger hidden all these years. That's probably the way to carry on.

Ralph: [*Ralph looks pensively into the middle distance and nods agreement. After a few moments he looks up.*] Yes, yes. I think so.

Counsellor: It's time now for us to finish. To say goodbye.

The counsellor pauses, allowing Ralph time to assimilate everything. She has done some important things:

◆ recognized the difficulty of his situation
◆ stroked him, thereby valuing his experience
◆ explained why and how to rebind his anger.

When she judges the moment right she will ask Angela to go back to her own chair and derole from Ralph.

Angela's reflections

Counsellor: Are you ready to talk as yourself, as Angela?

Angela: Yes.

Counsellor: What do you feel about what your father has shared?

Angela: I feel sorry that things turned out the way they did for him.

Counsellor: He sounded angry about it towards the end.

Angela: Mmmh. I'm not surprised really. Having to put a brave face on and pretend to feel OK must have made it even more difficult.

Far from being upset by her father's anger, Angela finds it understandable. Her counsellor is surprised and pleased at her response. It appears that her strategy has been effective. Angela has allowed her Parent ego state to become dominant to the exclusion of her other ego states. Phenomenologically, she became her internalized father, thinking and speaking as she would usually perceive him in her internal dialogue. By speaking her dialogue aloud, Angela is impacted in a new way by her own Parental thoughts and feelings; she can see things from a new perspective, and she has a witness to these in her counsellor. Speaking something in front of a witness adds impact to what is said, and makes later denial or minimizing less likely.

What about Angela's father's reaction in the here-and-now?

Of course, the change in Angela's internal experience may not be matched by a similar change in her real father as he is today. It will be very important to discuss the difference between the shift in her internal reality and the external reality. Her real-life father may well stick with his original views in the face of any changes Angela makes about her working life. Angela has control of her internal world. She does not have control over other people. She needs protection. To give her this protection the counsellor needs to ensure Angela has a strong grasp of the difference between the internal and the external. The counsellor will spend time in further sessions talking with Angela about these differences. Angela's internal world has changed but the people in her outer world are unlikely to show the same changes. She must help Angela to be ready to deal with whatever reaction her parents may have in the face of her changed priorities and new choices. The counsellor must provide ongoing support through this critical phase as Angela seeks to re-establish herself in her family. Angela may be bruised and hurt by family reactions or she may be delighted by them. At this point there is no way of knowing what will transpire. Learning to cope with whatever comes is part of Angela's task. If she is to become true to her own needs she has to be able to be resilient in the face of family responses.

The Child's world

Preparing for the Child's story

The Child stores experiences in an impressionistic form. When we move into Child our thoughts, feelings and bodily sensations are re-experienced in the same way in which we first experienced them. The story our Child carries is not a coherent narrative, it has not been reassessed in the light of Adult reality; rather, it shows us snapshots of our past experience. At their extremes, these may feel vague, impressionistic and tantalizingly beyond our grasp. Or they may be strong, powerful and shocking in their impact. Between these extremes lies a range of possible experiences. Some Child experiences are beyond language. We feel them as bodily sensations or emotional reactions, but we cannot understand what first caused them or where they link in with our past. Others have a much sharper cognitive focus and we can connect them to past circumstances and events. The Child carries a confusing wealth of experience which appears linked only in as much as it belongs to our own history.

To recapture spontaneity the inner Child needs to express what she carries. She needs to be helped to make sense of what she feels, clarifying confusion and integrating experience. It would be unsafe for the Child to come out if there was a possibility of retaliation by the Parent. That is why it is generally preferable to work with the Parent first: it protects the Child by giving the Parent an opportunity to be heard and seen. This makes it safer for the Child to show itself without fear of retribution or punishment. This is an essential aspect of providing protection for the Child.

The Child also needs permission to express itself freely, to show what she feels to the counsellor, without feeling inhibition. The counsellor's job is to help the Child to re-experience past circumstances which are repetitively unhelpful or intrusive. The client relives these in order to highlight the problem areas that need bringing out and working through so that they no longer impede spontaneous and authentic functioning. This is a very powerful thing to encourage someone to do and it is essential to check that the Child feels both safe and ready, and isn't fearful of Parent reprisals. Checking can be done in a straightforward manner, either by talking directly with the Child ego state and asking whether she feels ready for the next step, or by using the Adult as an intermediary and checking the inner Child's readiness through the Adult. Going through the Adult is preferable if there any concerns about readiness. It prevents any unbinding of Child energies and protects the Child from entering an internal emotional state for which they may not be ready, or which could be likely to prove unhelpful.

The Child's story

Facilitating the Child's story begins with the client entering their Child. This may occur spontaneously or it may be necessary to facilitate the process with some technical help, as in the Parent dialogue, using an empty chair to initially represent the Child, whilst the client sits opposite in Adult and actively imagines the Child, describing this to the counsellor. A gradual shift from Adult to Child will occur with this technique. When the client's energy is clearly with the Child they are ready to change chairs and move fully into Child experience. When this happens they will look and sound like the child that they were. It is important that the counsellor uses vocabulary to match the age of the Child. The counsellor will need to make their own judgement about whether or not it is necessary to use the empty chair technique. The method of facilitation is decided totally on the basis of which is most effective for the client.

Case example: Angela

Angela found it easy to move into her Child ego state. She described a childhood where everyone 'fussed' her; she was the centre of attention in the family. Family talk in the evening would frequently focus on her, her school day, her friendships, listening to her recite lessons for the next day, making new dresses for her. She provided a constant source of interest and delight. Her family were very protective, and if something was troubling Angela then everyone became troubled. At such times she would hear people talking in hushed voices about what could be done to make things better.

As Angela talked in general terms about her early years she became less animated and more reflective. It was obvious that her feelings were changing.

Angela: They're all trying so hard to be nice. But I just want them to leave me alone. I feel like I can't move or breathe. If I'm not happy I have to hide it. I have to pretend everything is OK. I feel so guilty if I make them worry. I want to make them happy. [*Angela suddenly moves back to here-and-now.*] I can feel it now, a sort of terrible churning in my stomach and this hot feeling. It feels like being slowly gripped tighter and tighter, until . . . until . . . until . . .

Angela's breathing was becoming very laboured, she was obviously struggling to catch her breath. Her face had become very red and her palms were covered with beads of sweat. She was close to a panic attack. Her counsellor acted quickly, handing Angela a paper bag; she directed her to place it over her nose and mouth so that she was breathing in and out of the bag. Talking calmly, she encouraged Angela to take slightly deeper breaths so that she stopped snatching breath. The effect of this and breathing in her own carbon dioxide soon worked. Angela began to breathe more easily, and was able to stop using the bag.

Counsellor: You started to panic as you recalled your feelings. Was that frightening?
Angela: Yes – very. I don't remember ever doing that as a child, it seemed stronger than I remember.
Counsellor: Is this how you used to feel in the office?
Angela: Yes. It never got this bad, but it always felt like it might.

What happened in the Child dialogue?

Angela has made a major discovery: she has discovered the historical source of the worrying panic attacks she has been having at work. This is a huge breakthrough. The internal source of Angela's hitherto inexplicable and confusing behaviour has finally been identified. The tension and anxiety she felt over many years as her family made her the constant focus for their attention has caused Angela's panic. She felt suffocated by their attention and trapped into trying to please them at the expense of her own spontaneous choices. With hindsight, Angela recognized the antecedents of the symptoms she had had at work in her Child experience. The Child, confused by the dilemma of trying to please the family at the same time as wanting to follow the right course for itself, became overloaded and stopped being able to function under the strain. The symptoms Angela first brought to counselling were the outcome. The root cause of the problem Angela first brought to counselling has been identified and *crystallized*.[3]

The Child dialogue has revealed why Angela is finding it so hard to function in a mature way where her family is concerned. The pressure of constantly wanting to please them and protect them from anything they would find disappointing places crippling constrictions on Angela, and she then stays in a child-like state around them ('don't grow up' injunction), not thinking about herself clearly ('don't think' injunction). Angela's increased awareness will enable her to think more clearly about herself and to understand her feelings and her choices better. A clear boundary will now exist between her Child experiences and her Adult reality.

Why was Angela's reaction in the counselling room stronger than it had been either at work or at home in childhood?

Sometimes, when the Child feels the safety of the counsellor's presence holding and containing, they stop trying to suppress their symptoms. Because there is no attempt to try and control the symptoms, they emerge with their full power.

Angela was really able to let go and give in to the full impact of her feelings, trusting in the protective skill and knowledge of her counsellor.

This is the first step for Angela in resolving the impasse where she gets stuck between pleasing her family and pleasing herself. Although the work will not be complete until the impasse is resolved, an important first step has been taken towards this resolution, with Angela courageously exploring the depth of her emotional conflict and allowing herself to feel both the emotional and the physical impact of this conflict. Once she has had time to stand back from her experience and reflect on what she found out, a significant strengthening of the boundary between Adult and Child will arise from Angela's increased awareness. The power of the awareness at this phase in the counselling is that is an *integrated awareness* deriving from combined emotional and cognitive knowledge, rather than just intellectual understanding. If her Child energies threaten to overwhelm her again, which they are quite likely to do, Angela will be less frightened. She will be able to have confidence in her capacity to withstand even a full-blown panic attack; she will have a much better understanding of what is happening; and she will have increased internal resources to contain and rebind her Child energies. Over time, and with further work, Angela will find her symptoms steadily diminishing, like watching a point on the horizon become steadily smaller and smaller until the final moment when it disappears from view and is lost forever.

Putting it all together: processing and integrating

It is crucial to spend time helping the client to assimilate both the Parent and the Child ego state work. This assimilation needs to take place in Adult so that the client creates their own reality-based understanding of themselves and their history. This new, up-to-date, reality carries with it a powerful authorization from the counsellor, who, in witnessing and supporting our struggle and fighting alongside us for our right to be self-defining, gives permission to hold our changed perceptions. This is more powerful than an out-of-date introjected Parent figure.

To help the client achieve integration, the counsellor must spend time discussing the sense they have made of the work they have done. The counsellor needs a clear picture of how her client has understood the work. Spending time on Adult *integration* allows the client time to reflect on and process her experiences. It gives time to sit back and take stock of the new realizations. It also allows the counsellor an opportunity to hear directly the client's view of her work. Occasionally clients may draw conclusions from the work that are based on a confused understanding. Discussing the work in this way gives the counsellor an opportunity to help the client correct any such misunderstandings.

Case example: Angela

Counsellor: Now that you've had some time to reflect on the work you've done, Angela, how are you feeling about it?

Angela: It's hard to describe really. In one way I don't feel any different, but at the same time I also feel much lighter inside. I still can't believe the reason for my panicking at work was so simple.

Counsellor: The source of your distress was easy to understand once you discovered it, but not so straightforward to find initially.

Angela: Yes, I suppose that's true.

Counsellor: Once the root cause of a problem is laid bare it can seem so understandable that you may lose sight of the complex path to finding it.

Angela: It does look obvious.

Counsellor: If you look back on all the work that led up to your realization, you can see that it was a far-ranging and complex journey. You have had to put in a lot to reach this point.

Angela: [*nodding*] It's easy to forget, isn't it?

Counsellor: It's important to fully value yourself and the work you've done. How do you look back on the Parent dialogue work you did?

Angela: It was amazing, wasn't it? All that stuff that just came out.

Counsellor: Yes. Now you have had a chance to listen in, as it were, on your own inner dialogue and hear it differently, you have more freedom to choose your direction because you know what comes from you and what comes from other people in your life.

What happened in the processing and integrating?

Angela was obviously in danger of denigrating her Child ego state work by telling herself that her discoveries were obvious. She was on the verge of using the work to further criticize and punish herself. Her counsellor intervened to help her appreciate the depth and complexity of the journey which had taken her to her new awareness.

Angela found it easier to accept her Parent ego state work. It didn't have a route back to any identifiable situation and she was surprised by the content of what emerged. She was clearly intrigued by what she discovered and found it easier to accept.

In future sessions Angela will go on to look at related issues that need to be worked through to complete her contract. But for now Angela has clarified her internal confusion and is well on the way to recapturing spontaneity and intimacy.

Summary

In this chapter we have explored how the client can reclaim greater Adult functioning and thereby make more sense of who they are today. This process of exploring the past through re-experiencing releases energy which can now be used more effectively to problem solve and fulfil their potential. The client is ready to move on to use these resources to free themselves from the chains of the past through the resolution of the impasse.

Key concepts in this chapter are:

♦ confusion

♦ impasse

♦ integrated awareness

♦ integration into Adult.

Key skills we have used are:

♦ questioning

♦ crystallization

♦ permission, protection, potency

♦ Parent dialogue

♦ Child dialogue

♦ reworking internal Child beliefs.

Exercises

Take a partner for these exercises.

7.1 Your partner role plays a client for whom Parent dialogue work is appropriate. Give your partner the necessary background information and then practise Parent dialogue, working from Adult to Parent and back to Adult.

Discuss your strengths and areas for further development.

Pay particular attention to you potency in working with the Parent. How did you come across? Is there anything you need to develop to enhance your potency? (Exercise time: 30–40 minutes.)

7.2 Your partner role plays the same client, this time telling their Child's story. Practise facilitating the Child's story, working from Adult to Child and back to Adult.

Discuss your facilitation with your partner and identify three learning goals. (Exercise time: 30–40 minutes.)

7.3 Discuss with your partner some crystallizing statements you could offer the client from your experience of the previous role plays.

Notes

1   E. Berne, *What Do You Say After You Say Hello?* (Corgi, London, 1974/1987), p. 374: 'Now we can speak with some assurance of the "three P's" of therapy which determine the therapist's effectiveness. These are potency, permission and protection. The therapist must give the Child permission to disobey the Parental injunctions and provocations. In order to do that effectively, he must be and feel potent: not omnipotent, but potent enough to deal with the patient's Parent. Afterwards he must feel potent enough, and the patient's Child must believe he is potent enough, to offer protection from the Parental wrath.'

2   J. McNamara and C. Lister-Ford, 'Ego states and the psychology of memory', *Transactional Analysis Journal*, 25, 2 (1995), pp. 141–9.

3   E. Berne, *Principles of Group Treatment* (Grove, New York, 1966), pp. 245–7: 'A crystallization is a statement of the patient's position from the Adult of the therapist to the Adult of the patient . . . If the patient is properly prepared by what has gone before, then his Adult will receive the crystallization eagerly and enthusiastically . . . At this stage the patient's Adult and Child are on good terms with each other, and the Child will also receive the crystallization gratefully, but with some trepidation and perhaps nostalgia as well, since it means abandoning permanently the old way and trying something new, still strange and not fully tested.'

Further reading

Crystallization

Berne, E. (1966) *Principles of Group Treatment*. New York: Grove. pp. 245–7.

Impasse

Mellor, K. (1980) 'Impasses: a developmental and structural understanding', *Transactional Analysis Journal*, 10 (3): 213–20.

Integration into Adult

Clarkson, P. and Gilbert, M. (1988) 'Berne's original model of ego states', *Transactional Analysis Journal*, 18 (1): 20–9.

Parent reconciliation

Dashiell, S.R. (1978) 'The parent resolution process: reprogramming psychic incorporations in the parent', *Transactional Analysis Journal*, 10 (4): 289–94.

Reworking internal Child realities

Clarkson, P. and Fish, S. (1988) 'Rechilding: creating a new past in the present as a support for the future', *Transactional Analysis Journal*, 18 (1): 51–9.

8 · Sustaining Intimacy

Intimacy is the willingness to be open and vulnerable with those we care about. It is to risk sharing what we really feel, think and want. It is to show ourselves as we really are – whether that is loving, angry, despairing, bored, restless, with strong views, with mild views, or not interested at all. From those we love, we want respect, acceptance and love in return. We want them to like enough of what they find in us to be able to tolerate those things they don't like so much. In return we offer back these same gifts of love, acceptance, respect and tolerance. Finding real intimacy requires the ability to be discerning, to know how to choose those we can truly trust. Intimacy is about committed, enduring connectedness. It is about riding the highs and lows without giving up and going off in search of momentary excitement or gratification because things aren't going the way we want. It requires the capacity to be fully present in the moment and, at the same time, to see beyond that moment.

Even the most script bound of us is capable of intimate moments – brief snatches of real closeness that are not ensnared in psychological game playing. This phase of counselling is about more than brief moments of intimacy; it is about developing the capacity to sustain intimate relating by working through any remaining symbiotic patterns that are preventing this. This is risky. Your client must confront those things in herself and in her nearest and dearest that are getting in the way. Understandably, this raises fears and anxiety. Will our relationships survive the challenge? Or will we be left high and dry without anyone?

The counsellor treads a delicate path: on the one hand, responding with empathic reassurance to contain these understandable worries; and, on the other, providing encouragement and help to work through fixed symbiotic patterns.

The counsellor's goals are to:

◆ specify and crystallize the client's symbiotic pattern

◆ specify and crystallize the predominant impasse conflict

◆ soothe and contain the client's fear and anxiety.

At the completion of the work, your client will:

◆ have broken relevant symbiotic patterns

◆ have resolved their predominant impasse conflict

◆ be able to sustain intimate relating.

Healthy intimate relationships

Healthy adult relationships are characterized by feelings of trust and security. Intimate relationships, where we are closely attached to someone special, provide the bedrock of our security in life. We feel safe to be ourselves in the relationship. Both partners are able to be mutually interdependent, relying on each other in a fluid, free-flowing way. From time to time, one or the other may move into mild dependence but does not become stuck there, and easily moves out again. The individuality of both people has room for expression and is nurtured by the relationship. On the whole, it is safe to experiment with ways of being. There is no need to worry that we will seriously threaten our loved one if we show who we are and what we are capable of. We do not fear rejection or that our partner will withdraw and leave us stranded without their love and support if we express our spontaneous and unique individuality. Feeling accepted helps us to accept and cherish the uniqueness of our partner without becoming unduly threatened, intimidated, anxious or envious of them and their abilities.

When changes occur in the relationship these may feel challenging because our secure base is being changed and, therefore, there is an inevitable sense that it is being challenged. Inevitably, this throws up ripples of anxiety and a variety of feelings that need to be talked through. In sustained intimate relationships people can allow change to take place in each other and they can work through the challenges this presents.

Is sustained intimacy possible with more than one person?

The short answer is 'yes'. However, there are definitely a finite number of people with whom we can sustain intimacy. Intimacy is emotionally demanding and time consuming. Our emotional well-being and sense of connectedness is necessarily shared with a chosen few – a partner, a special friend, close family.

Symbiosis

Childhood symbiosis

Children need to rely on their parents to support, nurture and protect them as they make the long and complex journey to maturity. Healthy childhood symbiosis is a biologically determined survival strategy that bonds parent and child in a powerful emotional and physical union. This bond, like a protective shield, is fluid and flexible; it is intended to help the developing child experiment with their abilities, skills and knowledge. The symbiosis must never smother the child, nor should it be so tenuous as to arouse fears of abandonment. In either case the child would lack the right kind of support to try out new facets of his own nature or experiment with life. He would therefore not gain the necessary confidence in himself to manage his own difficulties or negotiate life's ups and downs. As the child moves from one milestone to the next the intensity of the symbiotic bond should imperceptibly diminish until, by adulthood, symbiosis gives way to a new kind of bond between the child and his mother, which recognizes the child as a mature and independent young adult. The symbiosis has served its purpose and can now be sloughed off like a skin that needs to be shed.

Symbiosis in adults

Symbiosis occurs when two individuals behave as though they constituted a single person. Each person in a symbiosis is discounting certain ego states so that only one Parent, Adult and Child is functioning.[1]

Symbiosis in adults is usually unhealthy. Symbiotic relationships are characterized by:

◆ the limitations they place on us

◆ the way they constrain us to behave in predictable, set ways

◆ the way they limit creativity, spontaneity and flexibility.

However, let's not get carried away with ideas of perfection. Most adult relationships are symbiotic to some degree. An inevitable part of entering a relationship is a willingness to relinquish some of our wants and needs in the interest of making room for the other person with their wants and needs. In this process it is inevitable that sometimes we swing too far in one direction and then need to redress the balance. Problems occur when we cannot redress that balance and we get stuck in a position that requires us to keep aspects of ourselves repressed.

Example: functional symbiosis

Amanda disliked cooking, she found it stressful. Keith enjoyed cooking but loathed tidying up – something Amanda did well. Keith and Amanda came to an understanding that Keith would do most of the cooking and Amanda would do most of the 'tidying up', from simply putting things away to polishing shoes and remembering to launder the clothes.

This *functional symbiosis*, where Amanda and Keith have agreed to apportion tasks (or functions) based on their abilities and preferences, is made by agreement and with full awareness. It is useful and helps them to function more fluently. If there is a need they can take on the other's tasks.

Deciding which symbiotic patterns to work through

The task of the counsellor is to decide, with the client, which symbiotic patterns are key to the counselling contract and must be worked through if the goals of the counselling are to be attained.

Two factors are particularly helpful in this decision-making process. The first is the work that has gone before in discovering internal confusion (see Chapter 6), which will have revealed a great deal about problem symbiotic patterns. The second, and perhaps more helpful, is the symbiotic pattern that is evident in the way the client relates to the counsellor.

Symbiosis in the counselling relationship

Symbiosis from client to counsellor

Clients seek to make relationships with their counsellors that are based on their internal patterns of relating. The client tries to apply these 'rules' of relating to the counselling. This is not done with deliberate intention. Clients are usually unaware of this. However, from the counsellor's point of view, this attempt to superimpose their symbiotic patterning on the counselling relationship is a gold mine, rich in information about the client. It provides the counsellor with:

◆ valuable information which straightforward inquiry would not reveal (because the client is not aware of their behaviour and would not be able to easily articulate it)

◆ first-hand experience of how the client behaves in relationships

◆ first-hand emotional reactions to the client which are useful in gauging how the client is likely to impact other people.

The counsellor must also decide how she will work with this rich source of material. Some TA counsellors prefer simply to use it as a way to inform their own understanding. Others use it more explicitly with the client, bringing it overtly into the relationship as a way of focusing on building awareness by helping the client to notice the expectations they carry and are transferring onto the relationship. Whichever general direction you prefer to follow, no longer-term piece of therapy can be complete, as we shall see in Chapter 9, until the symbiotic disappointments and subsequent therapeutic failures have been worked through. These are an inevitable byproduct of the therapist relating to the client in a game-free way and therefore not responding according to the client's scripted internal hopes, fears and expectations. Unfinished business is the unseen driving force which compels the person, outside awareness, to seek out other individuals who will play the complementary hand in the psychological games that will further their script. The symbiotic relationship binds these individuals together in an initially rewarding but ultimately disappointing game-ridden bond.

Deciding how to use the symbiosis from the client

Here are some pointers to bear in mind when deciding how to use symbiosis.

First, symbiosis can be used exclusively to inform your own understanding. Do this if:

◆ the work can proceed just as effectively this way

◆ sharing will cause a negative reaction in your client – for example, feeling one down, ashamed, stupid, or angry.

Do not do this if:

◆ any of the positive indications below apply.

Second, symbiosis can be brought into the counselling relationship. Do this if:

◆ it will facilitate your client's self-understanding

◆ by working through their symbiosis with you it will help your client do this more effectively in their life

◆ the symbiosis between you cannot be ignored for some reason – for example, because it is preventing the counselling moving forward.

Do not do this if:

◆ it will confuse your client

◆ it will give your client unnecessary work

◆ it will generally 'muddy the water'

◆ it is to meet your own need to share your understanding of what is happening between you.

Moving beyond symbiotic patterns

To recapture her internal truth, your client must move through and beyond her symbiotic patterns. This is the path to intimacy. Earlier on in the work, you will have specified key problem areas (Chapters 5 and 6); the task now is to facilitate the next steps in moving through symbiosis.

Case example: Angela

Angela became anxious when she began to think about separating from her parents. She felt worried that she would cause them irreparable hurt by 'abandoning' them and going her own way. She continued to feel guilty when she considered letting go of the role her family had given her as 'the eternal child who made everyone feel better'. She worried that she would no longer be loved or accepted in the same way.

Angela's counsellor acknowledged how difficult it was to take such a step. She was *empathic* and *containing*, allowing Angela to wrestle with the problem over several sessions. In one session, as Angela was struggling she became unexpectedly angry with her counsellor.

Angela: You never told me it would be this difficult. I don't feel I'm getting any help from you. You just sit there agreeing with everything I say. How am I supposed to know what to do? It's easy for you. You just sit in that chair and say nice things. You've no idea what this feels like, if you did you would give me some real help like you used to. I don't think you care any more.

The counsellor recognized that Angela was feeling insecure and because of this believed the relationship had changed. Her anxieties with her counsellor parallel her anxieties about her family:

◆ She fears her counsellor cares less for her than she did previously.
◆ She is projecting onto her counsellor her fear that her family will love her less if she changes. This is symbiotic.

Angela rarely expresses anger because of her belief that she must please others and adapt to their needs. Her anger towards her counsellor is a really important milestone on the path to regaining intimacy by placing her own demands on a relationship. How her counsellor responds at this time is very important.

Her counsellor responded by helping Angela to express and understand her anger, her fears and her dissatisfactions. Together, they explored her perception that the relationship had changed. Gradually Angela was able to recognize that her fears and anxieties about her family were colouring her perception. In fact her counsellor was not responding in any significantly different way. Angela was taking the first step in relinquishing her symbiosis by challenging her counsellor and expressing her dissatisfactions, wants and needs. Enabling Angela to work this through in the counselling relationship is a forerunner of her being able to do the same with her family.

Angela has reached a very tender phase. Her counsellor must tread gently in coming sessions, supporting her to speak from her true self so that she gains in confidence. It is essential to ensure that Angela has ample opportunity to say how she is finding the counselling, to help her continue to build her confidence in speaking her real thoughts and feelings.

In time, when she feels ready, she can focus on the next step in relinquishing the symbiosis, looking at making a new place for herself in her family by giving up the 'eternal child' role in favour of her own mature identity. This second phase of working with the symbiosis with her family will need careful pacing, gentleness and sensitivity; it will bring up powerful feelings that will be painful and difficult to contain, plunging Angela into anxiety once again.

Key skills

◆ Take extra time to reflect on your responses.
◆ Be patient.
◆ Facilitate your client to express and make sense of her real feelings.
◆ Stroke any attempt to move in the direction of intimacy.

Impasse resolution

No symbiosis can be resolved until the impasse underpinning it has been resolved. An impasse occurs when we experience conflict between script messages on the one hand and our real feelings and desires on the other. We experience 'stuckness' which arises from the meeting of an irresistible force – our authentic desires which keep pushing for recognition and expression – with an immovable object, the script command, which does not want to give up its dominance. Generally, most of us deal with this kind of conflict by allowing one side to have its way. And then, briefly, the feeling of conflict is removed, the stuckness temporarily abates and we feel immediate relief. There is, however, a price to pay for one side gaining the upper hand. The aspect that did not get what it wanted feels thwarted and begins to reassert itself even more strongly, and so the battle builds and the feeling of conflict begins all over again.

What is an impasse?

In ego state terms, an impasse is a conflict between Parent and Child, between what has been introjected and what is spontaneously wanted or needed. Three types of impasse have been identified:[2]

◆ *Type 1* Generally developed in later childhood through internalizing verbal instructions (counterinjunctions) such as 'please others', 'try hard'. These are most accessible to awareness as the person can usually easily recall how they were delivered and by whom.

◆ *Type 2* Internalized in early childhood, often through non-verbal commands or cues. Based on injunctions such as 'don't grow up', 'don't feel'. Not so easily recalled as to how they were developed; however, the person can usually identify with the impasse conflicts.

◆ *Type 3* The earliest form of impasse, usually, but not exclusively, developed during the pre-verbal phase. Here the conflict is held in the body through tensions and psychosomatic complaints, or may be experienced through symbolic images and language, for example, 'I feel as if I am in a fog, lost, cold and alone.'

Figure 8.1 demonstrates this within the ego-state model.

Often, an impasse does not belong to us alone, but has already been felt by other members of our family at some time. As we have seen, script messages are generally passed down through the generations, with families unconsciously requiring different members to take on particular roles, attitudes and lifestyles. It is likely, therefore, that other generations have felt caught in the same dilemmas we face and have not known how to solve these. Equally, if we solve the impasse, will we upset the applecart by trying to introduce new ways that are alien in our family, culture or partnership? Will we feel rejected or scorned for daring to try something different? Or perhaps we will find that we no longer feel at home with people and circumstances that used to feel as though they fitted us perfectly.

These are dilemmas to which we cannot predict the answers. We will only discover the outcome if we risk the action.

What does it mean to resolve an impasse?

The counsellor must decide which impasse needs to be worked with. Some TA counsellors would seek to work systematically with all three types of impasse, but in reality it is often hard to separate them in this way. What often occurs in practice

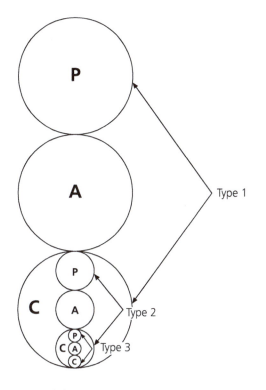

Figure 8.1 Impasse model

Adapted from the impasse model in 'Impasses: A Development and Structural Understanding' by Ken Mellor, originally published in the *Transactional Analysis Journal*, Volume 10, Number 3, pp. 213–20, 1980. Reprinted here with permission of Ken Mellor and the International Transactional Analysis Association.

is that when clients feel stuck they are generally experiencing all levels of impasse; their experience is not separated out into types but, in terms of the model, is conflated. Any experience of impasse conflict therefore usually describes all three theoretical aspects and is generally best being treated as such. Trying to separate out levels of experience often means artificially trying to bracket off aspects of the client's experience in a way that would fail to take account of the whole picture.

Impasse resolution requires the client to find a way to dissolve their script messages and comfortably assert their real wants and needs so that they fit the here-and-now reality of their lives. This is a difficult task, which takes time and practise. Resolving an impasse is the biggest kind of psychological upheaval we can be involved in. Everything gets thrown into the battle which rages between authenticity and script, insecurity, fear, anxiety, and feelings of aloneness, guilt and despair. Resolving an impasse requires psychological stamina, which means a good solid Adult ego state together with the motivation and 'grit' to stay the course. We have to be able to withstand feeling anxious, disoriented and vulnerable. We cast off from familiar and well-trodden shores, and like the early explorers who had only the stars and their knowledge to guide them, we have no surety of when or how we will arrive. We are sailing uncharted waters, and once we set off there is no going back; we can only go forward, placing our trust in our counsellor guide's knowledge that we will in fact arrive somewhere that we want to be – that the end is worth the journey.

Case example: Angela

Angela's impasse conflict combined a number of dilemmas:

◆ I have to please others at the expense of pleasing myself (type 1, 'please others').
◆ I want to live like a grown-up woman but I have to stay immature and dependent in order to be pleasing (type 2, 'don't grow up').
◆ I have overwhelming feelings of panic and anxiety when I contemplate really doing something I want to do (type 3, bodily reactions which 'paralyse' Angela, dull her thinking and prevent her from taking action).

With hindsight, we can see that Angela's presenting problems of panic and anxiety were an expression of her type 3 impasses. As she was feeling forced by her very real distress to look at leaving her job, she was brought up against the whole dilemma of whether she could act independently and make her own mature decision in accordance with her here-and-now adult need, or whether doing this would so displease her parents that she would feel the loss of her special place in their affections and in her family. Clearly, the conflicts of both the type 1 and 2 impasses are key parts of Angela's overall dilemma.

Recontracting with Angela

Angela's counsellor must initiate a new phase of contracting, in which she clearly spells out the difficulties that Angela is likely to encounter in this next phase of work. She must discuss honestly the range of emotions Angela is likely to feel, the difficulty of predicting how long it will take to complete impasse resolution, and the changes this could bring about in her relationships with her family. It is essential that Angela takes time to reflect, both with her counsellor and on her own, on the nature of the work she will be engaging in, so that if she decides to do the work she has given her full, informed consent.

Angela's decision

In Angela's case it was particularly the return of her anxiety and the possible changes in her family relationships that needed considerable reflection. At this point in the counselling she has gained control of her anxiety. Inevitably, if she opens Pandora's box, her anxiety is likely to return as she battles head-on with all the issues she will be unbinding once again, albeit this time from a place of choice rather than circumstance. It is a tough decision for Angela. She can decide to stop at this point, knowing she has made vast changes already which include having a much better understanding of herself and a greatly improved capacity to manage her own feelings, but with the possibility that if things ever get really difficult again some of those script-driven feelings and responses may re-emerge. Alternatively, she can take risks in the hope that she will transform and transcend her script, emerging profoundly changed and with little possibility of her old patterns reasserting themselves.

Angela eventually decided to continue. Some clients choose not to. It is important that the counsellor does not try to influence the client either way, but respects the decision they make and strokes the client for making the decision that is right for them.

Focusing on the issue and facilitating the Child within to speak

Angela and her counsellor discuss how the work will proceed. After looking at some options, they decide that for Angela everything focuses in a very immediate way on her relationships with her parents and her siblings and how she emerges from the role of 'adored, but never-quite-grown-up, special child'. The counsellor suggests that they start by exploring what this role has meant to Angela over the years, and particularly the benefits (secondary gains) it has brought. Released by the implicit permission to say what she likes about her position in her family, Angela can, in fact, speak about the things she would be reluctant to relinquish without having to openly come out and say so directly. This makes it easier for her to admit there are aspects of her situation she wants to keep. Implicitly, she can admit she wants to 'have her cake and eat it' without being put in the exposing position of 'owning up' to this directly. The therapeutic advantage of this approach is that she is unlikely to become defensive or withhold, from feelings of embarrassment, key pieces of information. Angela becomes animated and talks freely about the feelings of safety and 'cosiness' she feels with her family.

Angela: I know that they are always there for me, always behind me. If ever I need anything I can just pick up the phone and they will stop everything until things are sorted out. It's a wonderful feeling; it makes me feel so safe. My friends envy the closeness I have with my family.

Angela's counsellor remained empathic, encouraging Angela to say more without in any way attempting to challenge her. Her intention was to facilitate in Angela as full an expression as possible of the benefits of the symbiosis with her family. She reasoned that by doing this, Angela herself would, when she was ready, start to express awareness of the downside of what she was describing. In ego state terms, it was important to give the Child maximum encouragement to express every-thing, without it feeling it had to hide anything. Anything hidden at this stage could remain as a pocket of resistance that could undermine things at a later date when Angela starts to bring out the negatives in her situation. If the Child tried to hold on to unexpressed feelings of pleasure, it could block a full exploration of the negatives and stop everything coming out into the open. As far as possible, this is to be avoided.

The process of the work

The first step in letting go: reminiscing and reflecting

Over the next few sessions Angela continued to reflect on and reminisce about her earlier life with her family. It became increasingly obvious, despite all the problems her upbringing had brought her as an adult, that she had a warm, supportive family who doted on her and loved her. There was no obvious conscious or delib-erate intent to hurt, in fact quite the opposite.

At one point Angela brought some photographs of a family holiday. As she looked at them with her counsellor she noticed that in nearly all of them she was in the centre of the picture. Seeing pictorially what she had been describing for so long had a great impact on her. She became sad and a few tears trickled down her cheek. She was starting to feel the full impact of what she was saying goodbye to, a position in her family, which although now stifling had once felt a warm safe haven.

The counsellor's reflections

After the session the counsellor reflected that the process was leading Angela to nat-urally feel her grief in the face of all that she would lose in saying 'goodbye'. It was painful to see Angela so distressed and momentarily tempting to want to rescue her from her feelings. Angela's family sounded like genuinely kind and loving people.

Perhaps there was a way in which something could be worked out which could leave the symbiosis marginally intact, protecting the family from any potential distress, but with Angela still free enough to live without too much constraint.

Suddenly, the counsellor realized what she was thinking. She felt shocked. What had possessed her to wander down such a sentimental path? In asking herself the question she began to see the answer. She was, in all likelihood, picking up on Angela's feelings and paralleling them. Angela was probably feeling not only sadness and grief, but some guilt as well about disappointing the very people who had loved and nurtured her. The counsellor needed to guard against her own collusion with this.

Feeling the pain

In the next session Angela was more distressed than she had been for a long time. She reported a number of disturbing dreams that had left her feeling worried, anxious and guilty. As Angela talked about her dreams and the feelings they evoked, it became obvious to her counsellor that they indicated the pendulum was beginning to swing and that Angela was now spontaneously starting to be in touch with the pain of her dilemma. She reflected to herself that her own previous sentimental protectiveness was probably an indication of Angela's last try at clinging on to the past, a final attempt at bargaining, before taking herself into the midst of the dilemma with all its pain and difficulty. In the following sessions, as Angela focused on her grief, her anxiety became foreground once more, as her counsellor had thought it would. It took every ounce of Angela's resolve to stay with things at this point. Her major preoccupation focused on her fear that the panic attacks of old would reappear and that she would be helpless to do anything about it. 'I'll be back to square one but with no hope of finding a solution this time.'

The breakthrough

As the counsellor continued exploring Angela's anxiety, something new began to emerge – underlying feelings of frustration and anger. Angela was beginning to feel 'suffocated' and 'constrained' by her family. She wanted to break free, to try out new things, to experiment with not having to achieve. Her perception of her family began to change; she now saw them as 'middle of the road, boring and banal': 'They pour sugar on everything to try to keep things sweet and expect me to do the same!' The breakthrough had come; Angela had finally reached beyond her anxiety and found what had lain buried for so long. Her outspoken words revealed a strong, healthy and vibrant capacity for spontaneity!

A delicate and important new phase had arrived in the counselling. Angela had never been through the normal teenage rebellion in which she could identify herself as an individual, different and separate from her parents. As she had said earlier, 'there was nothing to kick against'. The need to do this was emerging through the work of resolving the impasse as her suppressed anger bubbled out.

Protecting the client

At times like this, I often find it useful to remind my clients that 'now is not then'. We can be angry with people in the counselling room, but it is advisable to contain this in the world outside. If our clients take old anger toward parents (or anyone else) into their current relationship with them, this will only add to the difficulties and could be potentially damaging. Part of being able to hold Adult is the capacity to recognize that, in resolving old problems, those who caused us to feel wounded may be very different people today from the people they were then. And, even if they are not, until the work is complete and we have arrived at an integrated position within ourselves from which a mature, reflective decision can be taken, it is always best to hold back.

Expressing the incomplete developmental need

As Angela worked with her unmet need from her teenage years to kick against the traces (something which it is essential to do if we are to find a separate identity from our parents that is unique and also feels like it has been forged by our own efforts), she expressed many pent-up feelings with and at her counsellor. Her counsellor remained constant and supportive, knowing how vital it was that Angela felt as unquestioningly accepted in this phase of the work, when she was taking huge risks in expressing her spontaneity, as she had earlier on when she was not putting herself on the line in quite the same way. Angela's earlier anger with her counsellor when they were exploring her symbiotic pattern had been a prelude to this part of the work.

It was not always easy to remain unaffected and empathic. Sometimes, as with any teenage-type comment, Angela reached her mark and succeeded in arousing feelings of irritation. Her counsellor knew how vital it was not to let this show; she must *contain her own feelings*. She found giving vent to her feelings in supervision an invaluable way of safely letting off steam and ensuring that in the sessions she could be present without acting on her own feelings. Her supervisor's non-judgemental, supportive approach really helped her to use supervision in this way and did, of course, mirror her own approach with Angela. Cascading from the supervisor down, through the counsellor, to Angela herself was respect for the right of someone to voice his or her negative feelings and thoughts and to be listened to.

This permission, quietly but potently expressed, was the bedrock which gave Angela the opportunity to work through and resolve the pent-up (bound) feelings of which she had been unaware. She began to emerge from her anger and resentment with a new attitude towards both herself and her parents.

Meeting the here-and-now needs

Angela: I've decided I'm going to shorten my name. I like Angie. I've wanted to do it for years but my parents were against it. I just don't feel like an Angela anymore. Angie feels crisper, livelier and, more fun, than good, boring angelic Angela. I want you to call me Angie from now on.

I've made some other decisions, too. I don't remember if I told you, but about 18 months ago I was offered a job in Manchester. It was working in the same field but with a much more go-ahead company. I'd have more opportunity to develop my own ideas. I turned it down flat at the time; I didn't see how I could possibly go. The chap I spoke to gave me his card and said if I ever changed my mind to get in touch. I'm going to. It's just the kind of job I'd love to do. I don't know how my family will take it, but I won't let guilt about leaving them get in the way anymore. I want them to understand why I need to lead my own life and make my own decisions, but if they can't there's nothing more I can do about it.

The counsellor's reflections

Angie has reached internal integration. She had not, in fact, mentioned the job offer. It seemed so unattainable that she had not even thought it worth mentioning (internal discount). She has worked through her impasse, expressing her genuine anger, for which her anxiety was only a cover, and come to a place where she can keep firm hold of her own spontaneous desires, hoping her family will understand but not going to be put off if they don't. Her anger has matured into a capacity for reasoned and reasonable self-assertion that is sensitive to the needs of others but not swamped by them. Her determination has paid off. Her gamble has been worth it.

Comment

Angie has worked through three layers of impasse. By staying with the discomfort of her anxiety and panic (type 3) she has been able to discover the unexpressed and forbidden feelings of anger which lay underneath her 'don't grow up' injunction. Once she could express these she was able to grow into her own views, opinions and ideas – in short, to mature (type 2). Part of this maturing involved weighing up the pros and cons of giving up pleasing her family when the cost to herself was too great (type 1). The last part of resolving the impasse involved, as we saw, coming to the realization that pleasing herself was vital if she was to live a productive, creative and satisfying life. She retained her capacity for sensitivity to others but was no longer willing to put their needs first if it undermined her own well-being. The symbiosis with her family is broken. She can now look at how a new relationship can be built with them, which, from her own perspective, comes from a position of authenticity.

Angie's movement through her impasse conflict was unique to her story. Not everyone moves from type 3 to type 2 to type 1. Progress through the impasse types varies according to the individual's script, life circumstances and immediate needs. The counsellor must plan her strategy for facilitation based on how the client presents their difficulties and what is causing most discomfort. Every situation is unique. Similarly, not everyone can, or should, be understanding of or forgive the people who have hurt them and caused their pain. For example, where a client clearly has a toxic parent (or other relationship) such as in situations of gross abuse or neglect, part of impasse resolution may involve a decision to repudiate entirely the person and their actions. Each set of circumstances is different and the resolution the client wants and finds appropriate must be what determines the outcome.

Supervision pointers

Self-supervision

Working from what you have learned in this chapter, including the exercises at the end:

◆ Summarize your strengths and learning goals.

◆ Make a realistic plan for meeting your learning goals.

◆ How might you become caught up in the client's process?

◆ How would your effectiveness be undermined if this happened?

◆ If you have an instance of getting enmeshed with the client's situation then use this, or otherwise imagine a possible scenario, and consider how you could retrieve the situation.

Reflect on the quality of your relationship with your supervisor:

- What are the pros and cons of the relationship?

- How open are you with your supervisor?

- Is there anything either you or your supervisor could do to enhance the relationship?

Supervision with your supervisor

- On client material: talk with your supervisor about your thinking from your self-supervision.

- On your relationship with your supervisor: if you feel ready, share your reflections with your supervisor.

Summary

In this chapter we have focused on an overview of the process between counsellor and client that usually occurs within the relationship during this phase of the work when deep and unresolved conflicts come to the fore. To accommodate a variety of client situations we may need to draw from a range of techniques and interventions. Those commonly used in this stage are as follows:

- decontamination

- game analysis

- deconfusion

- ego state dialogue

- the Parent interview.

Important work has been accomplished with the resolution of symbiosis and impasse. Some of the deepest layers of script are almost resolved and autonomy is in sight. In the next chapter we look at the final stages of the work when the client practises putting it all together.

Key concepts in this chapter are:

- intimacy

- symbiosis

- impasse.

Key skills we have used are:

- patience

- empathy

- active reflection

- containment of the counsellor's feelings and reactions

- acceptance and containment of the client's feelings and reactions

- change in stroking pattern

- contract renegotiation

- active use of supervision

- working through symbiosis

- impasse resolution.

Exercises

Most of the exercises for Part Three involve you practising techniques that take longer to complete. I suggest you experiment with different exercises on different days so that you stay lively and give yourself time to consolidate your learning. Most exercises will take between 60 and 90 minutes.

You need a partner for these exercises:

8.1 *Permission, protection, potency*
  (a) Each selects a client with whom you are currently working. Give your partner a pen picture of the client, relevant intake data, presenting issues, a skeleton TA assessment, the contract and the current phase of the work. Practise making the information you give crisp and to the point.
  (b) Now each of you design a three-phase permission, protection, potency (PPP) set of transactions.

(c) In turn, each discuss your intervention strategy and make any useful modifications.

(d) In turn, role play your own client whilst your partner role plays the counsellor and makes the PPP transactions.

(e) After each role play, discuss how the transactions have felt to the 'client' and the 'counsellor'. Before you complete the discussion each time, be sure to summarize your learning points from both roles.

8.2 *Parent dialogue and reconciliation*

(a) Taking the same client, your partner continues in role whilst you practise Parent dialogue and, if possible, reconciliation.

(b) At the end of the work, talk through what came easily and what you found more difficult. Identify the next step in developing your skills.

(c) Swap roles.

8.3 *Reworking Child realities*

(a) In turn, each of you continues in the 'client' role as your partner practises working with the Child's realities.

(b) In your process discussion at the end, include time to look at how integration into Adult would be facilitated.

8.4 *Symbiosis*

This is a shorter exercise.

(a) Taking each client in turn, discuss his or her predominant symbiotic pattern.

(b) Make a plan of how you will help the client break their symbiosis. Discuss specific interventions you will use.

8.5 *Impasse resolution*

(a) Taking each client in turn, specify and diagram the predominant impasses. Diagram the three types and discuss their interrelatedness.

(b) Take each client in turn and discuss the stages in which the impasse conflict would be worked through. Make sure you have clear, focused reasons for your decision.

(c) In turn, role play the work with the client. After each piece of counselling practice, discuss the strengths and weaknesses of your approach. How might you modify it?

Notes

1   Tony Tilney, *Dictionary of Transactional Analysis* (Whurr, London, 1998), p. 120.
2   M. Goulding and R. Goulding, *Changing Lives Through Redecision Therapy* (Grove, New York, 1982), pp. 44–9. K. Mellor, 'Impasses: a developmental and structural understanding', *Transactional Analysis Journal*, 10, 3 (1980), pp. 213–21.

Further reading on impasse theory

Goulding, M. and Goulding, R. (1982) *Changing Lives Through Redecision Therapy*. New York: Grove. Chapter 3, pp. 44–9.
Mellor, K. (1980) 'Impasses: a developmental and structural understanding', *Transactional Analysis Journal*, 10 (3): 213–21.

Part Four

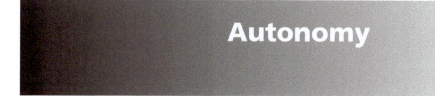

Autonomy

9 · Making the Transition to Autonomy

Synthesis and integration

Regaining autonomy is the final phase of the counselling journey. It is sometimes referred to as the 'relearning' phase.[1] It is the time when all that has been worked on throughout the period of counselling begins to appear in newly configured ways as the final internal synthesis between the old and new nears completion. Sometimes integration is solid and clear and sometimes gaps and flaws show up as script ways are left behind and tried and tested alternatives need to be fine polished. For your client this time will, overall, be positive, exciting and packed with anticipation and aspiration. The final stretch is in sight and there is often great eagerness to reach the finishing line. Changes made throughout the period of the counselling now seem to fit together in new ways, creating new patterns of understanding, feeling and experience. New internal relationships are created that bring together past learning. It is a time when awareness which has been gained earlier on is brought into connection with spontaneity and intimacy, as your client starts to practise putting it all together, actively and purposefully putting their 'new show on the road'.[2]

Excitement and despondency

Alongside the excitement that comes from the positive mastery of new ways, there are also times of anxiety when all does not go well and your client feels momentarily disheartened by their incapacity to manage things in the way they want to. 'Betwixt and between' often sums up how they feel at such moments when progress seems slow and painstaking. Frustration and disappointment momentarily swamp joy and excitement. Such moments are generally short lived providing the counsellor responds quickly and positively, mediating the client's anxiety and helping them to find and learn from the rich lessons that are always rooted in these times of trouble.

Attaining autonomy

> Parents, deliberately or unaware, teach their children from birth how to behave, think, feel and perceive. Liberation from these influences is no easy matter, since

they are deeply ingrained and are necessary during the first two or three decades of life for biological and social survival. Indeed such liberation is only possible at all because the individual starts off in an autonomous state . . . capable of awareness, spontaneity and intimacy, and he has some discretion as to which parts of his parents' teaching he will accept.[3]

The goals for this final phase are:

◆ to enable your client to integrate and synthesize an autonomous attitude

◆ to enable your client to practise new autonomous behaviours

◆ to support your client from the sidelines.

By completion of this phase you can expect that your client will:

◆ feel congruently autonomous

◆ feel confident using autonomous behaviours

◆ have developed strategies for moving out of any momentary dips into script behaviours.

The counsellor's task

Counsellor approach

The key task for the counsellor is to remain *constant* and *encouraging*. Although it may not always be obvious, the client is, in fact, at a very vulnerable juncture, and is still strongly dependent on you for constancy and encouragement. You need to be mindful that even at this late stage, failure to properly attune to your client and remain supportive and involved can result in serious therapeutic failure, leaving her lost in a no man's land somewhere between script and autonomy, devoid of the ability to go back and still without a fully tested path forward. Being constant means:

◆ staying calm

◆ stroking positive developments

◆ soothing anxiety, panic and despondency

- holding firm to your belief in your client's capacity to reach her goals

- remembering that she still needs you to stay with her to the end

- concentrating 100 per cent on every step she still has to take.

You must not slacken your attention or loosen your involvement until the client has closed the door on you for the last time.

Skills and techniques

Qualities of *interested inquiry* and *loving encouragement* are now more important than specific techniques, which largely belong to earlier phases of the counselling work. Now, it is the *quality of relationship with you* that sustains your client. It is her bond with you, the knowledge that you offer a safe harbour, where she can come and share the pleasures and pains of progress, protected by a veil of privacy, cushioned by your permissive support and encouraged by your potent belief in her abilities. As one client put it, 'I can count on you to put my best interest first and encourage me to reach for things even when I feel it's impossible.'

Preparing for the shift to full autonomy

As with all shifts, the aim is to make things as seamless as possible, whilst accepting that any change is bound to be a bit bumpy in places. As a counsellor, you will know when the time is right for the change from client cues. You may, for instance, find the client starting to describe more frequent examples of independent action that catch you slightly by surprise because they show new initiative in an area where formerly there was lack of awareness or fear to act. The client will become less reliant on you, less interested in discussing things beforehand and more likely to tell you after the event. Their discussions with you describe release from script-driven behaviours and show increasing confidence in their own opinions and belief in their own judgements.

The client is now ready to go through a period of *rapprochement* when they need to come and go.[4] They will be going off into the outside world, trying new things out and then coming back to share their successes, failures, fears and excitement with you. Above all, you must be there to come back to, to celebrate successes and to soothe failures. Your constancy is your client's safe harbour, vital in their building of self-confidence. They need confidence not only in their capacity to make the transition out of script but also in their own ability to ride the difficulties without fear that every rough patch spells the end. You need to help your client:

- learn that ups and downs are commonplace and to be expected

- gain an accurate and realistic impression of these new 'normal' life difficulties

- feel safe and at ease with her own capacity to negotiate these.

Gradually, she will begin to assume full and independent responsibility for her new, autonomous self.

Key skills

The skills required of the counsellor at this stage are:

- constancy
- interested enquiry
- encouragement
- positive stroking.

Orienting the client to what is ahead

Orienting your client to what is ahead is best accomplished through a variety of means:

- *explanation* of the new phase

- opportunities for *answering questions*

- *recontracting* in which the parameters of the work are talked over and agreed.

Case example: Angie

Angie's move into this last phase of her counselling was enthusiastic, determined and wholehearted. Her timidity of the early days was gone completely. She walked into her usual Tuesday afternoon session with her face lit by a huge beaming smile.

Angie: I did it! I rang him – the guy in Manchester. I've got an interview for the job in four weeks' time. I can hardly believe it, I can't stop thinking about it. Isn't it fantastic!
Counsellor: You sound excited. Congratulations!

As Angie described her conversation with her contact in Manchester, her counsellor saw that she had moved into a place of genuine autonomy. She was ready to move into the final phase of her counselling work. It was time to prepare for the eventual ending that was now moving into focus. Angie's counsellor decided to use her possible move to Manchester as the pivot from which to start the discussion.

Counsellor: This is a wonderful opportunity. Have you had a chance to think about the kind of changes this might bring?

Angie: It will be a big upheaval, I know. If I get the job I'll be the first one in the family to leave the area. I'll be like a pioneer.

Counsellor: You are already a pioneer.

Angie's expression became reflective as she took time to consider her counsellor's confrontation. The simple but powerful statement was designed to cut away any vestiges of script that could undermine Angie's Adult. Her counsellor wanted to make it absolutely plain that by battling her way through her script she had broken new ground and was a pioneer. She had already made it a reality. Her success in breaking out of script and becoming autonomous was not something in the future to be aimed towards but was something Angie had already achieved. It was the basis from which Angie was now preparing for her new life, a life where she would be independent of both her family and her counsellor.

After some moments of silence in which her expression indicated she was taking the confrontation on board, Angie continued:

Angie: I don't know what you'll think about this. I've been thinking about how much I've changed. More than I ever thought possible. And, well . . . really I'm . . . I'm nearly ready to end with you.

Angie's statement comes hard on the heels of the confrontation. Although there is some hesitancy and anxiety in her voice, she has clearly accepted the recognition of her autonomy made through the confrontation and is, in true pioneering form, breaking new ground with her counsellor. Angie is taking the ultimate step out of script in saying she wants to move on beyond the relationship. She is daring to put her own wants and needs first ahead of any consideration of her counsellor's feelings. This is the culminating moment of her whole counselling journey, the moment she and her counsellor have worked so hard together to achieve. Everything now hinges on the counsellor's response.

Counsellor: I've been thinking about that, too. I think you're right. You have made enormous changes – you've transformed how you feel about yourself and your life. And now you're about to transform the way you live your life. You are definitely putting the results of your counselling into practice in your life. You have new horizons ahead with new people and new places.

The client's needs

Angie's counsellor positively strokes her, following up Angie's statement with strongly supportive comments. She reinforces Angie's autonomous position, leaving no room for Angie to feel invited back into symbiosis. She gives 100 per cent unconditional backing to Angie's expression of autonomy. Angie has taken the kind of risk characteristic of true intimacy. She has expressed her own needs in a truthful and direct way, rather than resorting to script-driven symbiotic behaviours. She has shown real courage with her candid, game-free truthfulness.

The counsellor has framed the approaching ending as a positive step in Angie's development. In doing this, she has begun the bridging process between Angie's present situation and her future one by offering Angie a positive, upbeat frame into which she can put her own vision of the next phase of her life. Her counsellor supports Angie's reaching forward and outward beyond the confines of her existing circumstances towards the goals she has independently identified. Throughout her life, Angie has lacked sufficient encouragement to identify her own horizons. She has gained the impression from her family that she should limit her choices, tailoring them to meet family expectations, hopes and dreams – making real family dreams that others had failed to bring to fruition. Now Angie needs strong encouragement to make her own dreams real, to let go of other people's visions and to hold strongly to her own. Even a hint of regret or doubt from her counsellor could be really undermining at such an important and delicate moment.

Key skills

The skills required of the counsellor are:

♦ positive stroking
♦ supportive statements
♦ reinforcing autonomy
♦ recontracting.

Counsellor self-containment

What does the counsellor really feel?

This is also a delicate moment for the counsellor. As is so typical of this phase, Angie has surprised her and caught her off guard. Even though the counsellor knew this moment was very close she was still taken by surprise when it actually happened. The end of the counselling is now clearly in view. Angie's counsellor had a mixed response. She felt delight that Angie could say so clearly what she wanted, but she also felt a powerful sadness. She would miss Angie. Working with her had been a real pleasure. She was highly motivated and had made significant changes. Her counsellor felt enormous satisfaction in the work she had been able to accomplish with her. Letting go of the ease of relationship and depth of encounter was a real wrench. Her counsellor felt good about herself as a professional when she worked with Angie.

Supervisory help

In supervision, Angie's counsellor talked about her mixed response. Her supervisor helped her to recognize that she was caught up in Angie's script, that her feelings were, in fact, quite similar to those Angie had described in her own parents. Her supervisor enabled her to make a very important realization. Angie had described herself as a pleasing and rewarding daughter and now her counsellor was describing her as a client with those same qualities. The potential for responding to Angie from a parental script role had been a real possibility. The counsellor experienced a moment of shock when she saw how close she had come to the edge of her client's script. It reminded her of the need to be ever vigilant and that she must never take it for granted that her reactions were entirely without script significance. Better by far to assume this was a possibility until she had definitely ruled it out.

This was a real danger point in the counselling. Outside her awareness, there was a strong pull for Angie to return to script. If she herself were unaware, the counsellor could be the vehicle by which her client was pulled back into script.

As a means of preventing herself reinforcing Angie's script and as a way of supporting her own needs, Angie's counsellor talked with her supervisor about her sources of professional strokes and how Angie's leaving would alter the pattern. The counsellor realized she needed to look at the overall balance of her caseload in order to assess the way it would change. She would need to think carefully about her next referral in order to keep a right balance. Some of the important things to bear in mind when taking on a new client would include:

◆ Keeping a balance of different kinds of client problems so that there weren't too many of one kind which could become draining or repetitively dull.

◆ Keeping a balance of different kinds of client problems so that there are enough of a similar kind to provide continuity of style and approach; too many different client needs require a constant change of tempo and can be depleting.

◆ Predicting how the balance of strokes she gave and received in her working week was effected so that she didn't feel she was giving out so much that she became depleted, or receiving too many strokes of one kind, especially negative ones.

◆ Checking when clients were diaried so that there was both continuity and variety in the structure of her working week.

Key skills

The skills required of the counsellor at this point are:

◆ identify your emotional responses
◆ discuss endings with your supervisor
◆ focus on self-care
◆ review the impact on your caseload.

Case example: Angie

The counsellor's explanation

In their next session, Angie and her counsellor continued discussing what the changes were likely to bring. Her counsellor began to explain the new phase Angie had entered.

She described the opportunities it brought for Angie to put her new skills into practice in a real way. The prospect of a job interview for a post that would take her out of the area would allow her to test how competent and confident she felt in demanding circumstances. She would have a chance to find out how she coped, certain in the knowledge that her counsellor was waiting in the background, supporting her changes and ready to help with any problems that might arise. She emphasized how helpful it would be to have such a challenging situation in which to try out her new approach to life. In itself, the interview in Manchester was a positive opportunity. Any difficulties that Angie encountered could be talked through and solutions found. Going through such a big experience was a dress rehearsal for the time when Angie would be on her own once she had completed her counselling work. In attending the interview, Angie really would be taking risks and facing challenges as she aspired to reach her dream. But, on her return, she would still have direct and immediate access to help if she needed it.

As Angie's counsellor explained the process of finalizing her move into full autonomy and its benefit, Angie showed interest and asked several questions.

Angie's questions

Angie's questions focused on gathering information and settling the low level of anxiety she was feeling. She asked them over a couple of sessions, moving between her excitement, planning for the interview, and her anxiety. Her main ones were:

◆ How long is it likely to be before I move out of this phase?
◆ Do people ever find out that something crucial is missing that they have to come back and put right?
◆ If I get in a mess when I'm there, can I phone you?
◆ You would tell me if you thought I was fooling myself about being ready to do this, wouldn't you?
◆ How will I know when I'm ready to manage on my own? Do you just know?

Answering Angie's questions

Angie's counsellor decided that two different approaches were needed to answer her questions.

Some required *simple informative answers*. For example:

Angie: How long is it likely to be before I move out of this phase?
Counsellor: It's hard to be precise, much of that depends on you and how you feel. But you are clearly coming to the end.

With this approach, her counsellor wanted to use information as

◆ a means of empowerment to support Angie's strengthening autonomy
◆ a way of allaying her anxieties.

Some of Angie's questions required *indirect answers* because it was important for Angie to find her own answers once she was free of her worries. Working with her anxieties would clearly form part of the final work once the contract review was complete. To answer such questions directly at this point would probably only raise Angie's anxiety. For example,

Angie: If I get in a mess when I'm there, can I phone you?

To agree to allow Angie to phone if she felt upset would, of course, only support symbiosis and work against Adult. But to say so at this moment would disempower her Adult by stroking the Child fear. This could easily result in the Child taking over control from the Adult. *Rapprochement* requires small steps, taking things one at a time, going slowly. Becoming overwhelmed with anxiety about something that can be worked through slightly later would be counter-productive. Best to delay dealing with the content of the question until the underlying concern can be discussed and worked through. The way to answer the question is at a process level:

Counsellor: 'I can see that you are already thinking of strategies for solving any problems you encounter. That's a really positive thing to do. Let's look at the whole issue when you plan your trip.

In her answer the counsellor does a number of important things:

◆ She positively strokes the problem solving intention behind the request. Not only will this help Angie feel good about herself, but it is encouragement for her to continue using problem solving behaviours – something she will certainly need to be able to continue doing way past the end of the counselling.
◆ She intentionally shapes her client's helpful behaviours in a way that will facilitate optimal autonomy when Angie has finished counselling.

Answering Angie's questions led the way naturally to discussing and reviewing her contract.

Contract review

Reviewing the contract at this stage serves a number of essential purposes. It provides opportunities:

◆ to make explicit with your client her change in direction and to discuss together the significance of what is taking place
◆ to agree a plan for the remaining work
◆ for your client to give her informed consent
◆ to begin active preparation towards the ending.

This is the last big review that will take place in the work. It is a watershed. It gives your client a chance to really focus on what she wants and how she wants to go about it. It offers her a final opportunity to shape the direction of the work in order to achieve her goals.

Case example: Angie
Contract review

Angie wanted to work towards ending, irrespective of whether or not she got the job in Manchester. She recognized that her actions in securing an interview had been the catalyst for this. In letting herself know that she felt secure enough to take such a major step, she was also letting herself know that she was ready for another major step – ending counselling.

Angie and her counsellor decided on a two-phase contract. Angie's overall contract would focus on ending. The first phase of this would be to prepare for her interview. When she knew the outcome, then she would be in a better position to decide how to plan the second and last part.

Moving fully into the work

This follows hard on the heels of contract review. In practice, it generally flows directly on. Discussing the contract prepares the ground and the client usually moves seamlessly forward if the review has been effective.

Case example: Angie

Angie's earlier questions gave direction to the discussion. Her counsellor picked up on the underlying theme of anxiety that seemed to be motivating several of them. She had two goals:

1 to identify anxieties that were grounded in Child and help Angie formulate a way of soothing her Child
2 to identify genuine Adult concerns that anyone contemplating the changes Angie had in mind might feel and help her formulate strategies for addressing them.

Releasing Child worries

Angie's counsellor encouraged her to talk through her Child worries by starting with the question to which she had given an indirect answer. She didn't want to leave it longer than necessary to follow this up in case Angie's Child started to feel fobbed off and began generating fantasies about why the question had not been directly answered. The counsellor wanted her client to feel she had a place where she could bring her worries, confident of a sensitive response. By releasing negative Child energy, Angie's Adult would be able to take charge unimpeded, whilst her Child, because it felt heard and recognized, would feel reassured.

Angie talked freely about her fear that she had 'bitten off more than I can chew'. Going so far beyond the boundaries of her script had made her feel uneasy and she was responding with typical script anxiety of the kind which had, in the past, held her back from making autonomous decisions. Once she had expressed her fears she was able to see where they came from and recognize the false, contaminated view they represented. She could then move on to look at the Adult realities of the situation.

Addressing Adult concerns

Once her Child anxieties were allayed, Angie was able to concentrate on addressing how to confidently support herself from Adult as she went through the interview process. She realized that even if she got 'in a mess' whilst she was away, she would probably be able to deal with it. She talked through approaches to potential problems and in so doing recognized that she was an able thinker and strategist. She was able to put her concerns into perspective and see them as a normal part of such a ground-breaking venture. Angie decided spontaneously that asking to phone her counsellor came from an old place. She didn't need to cling to anyone's apron strings.

Angie's counsellor worked with her other anxieties in a similar way, showing sensitivity to her concerns, but refusing any invitation into a script symbiotic response. Instead, she worked to strengthen and reinforce her client's Adult and, therefore, her autonomy.

Key skills

The skills required of the counsellor at this stage are to:

◆ identify themes and plan the work around them
◆ give the Child the opportunity to talk
◆ identify strategies for supporting Adult
◆ be alert to 'last ditch' invitations into symbiosis.

Coming and going: autonomy in action

Each time your client seeks reassurance and feels her need has been met by you, she will gain in confidence. This will enable her to move ever closer to her own goals. Paradoxically, this means she will find it increasingly easy to move away from you. The more she is sure of your constancy, the less she will need to depend on your support, encouragement and confrontation. Increasingly, she will feel confident in her own judgements, feelings and opinions, and be able to reassure herself.

For the counsellor this is one of the most delightful times. After the hard work, careful planning and thoughtful interventions, you can take pleasure in stepping aside as your client puts her own 'show on the road'.[5] Your watchword is now 'support from the sidelines'. What does this mean? It means actively watching, waiting and encouraging – patiently allowing your client to go at her own speed as she enters the home run on her own.

Learning in your presence

In this final phase, learning in your presence is what your client needs to be able to do. It is an invaluable parting gift to offer your client for a number of reasons:

◆ It models belief in your client's ability to figure things out for herself when something goes wrong.

◆ It models making and correcting mistakes as a normal part of life and a rich source of learning.

◆ It is a powerful endorsement of your client's autonomy.

Pitfalls to avoid

Two of the main pitfalls to avoid are:

◆ 'helpful' responses

◆ an 'I saw this coming' reaction.

'Helpful' responses

One of the most crucial skills in this phase is suppressing any comment, however helpful or well intentioned, that would interfere with autonomy. Better by far to allow your client to make an error that they then have to figure out how to put right. We all learn from our mistakes. The prime educative function of an error is to teach us what doesn't work. This opens up the opportunity to:

◆ assess and analyse what we did

◆ to look at where our judgement was faulty

◆ to figure out why

◆ to look at what was needed instead.

These are precisely the skills your client needs to consolidate with you in this phase as a prelude to doing them alone once she has finished counselling. If you step in and rescue her from this valuable learning you will be doing her a disservice and denying her the opportunity to learn in your presence.

'I saw this coming' reaction

When your client comes to discuss something that has gone wrong, if you take an 'I saw this coming' attitude you will do her a great disservice. She may wonder why, if this is so, you did not warn her ahead. Are you taking covert delight in her difficulty? Do you secretly want her to fail? Are you failing to tell the truth when she asks for reassurance that she is ready for this final hurdle? Or perhaps you don't really want to let her go.

You have to allow your client to make errors and, when she comes to talk them through, keep your own counsel. Your job is to remain interested, enthusiastic and supportive of your client's approach without making a more direct intervention which would have suited an earlier phase of the work, but is now inappropriate and out of date.

What if I think my client may really cause herself harm?

If you believe something very seriously harmful could result from something your client is planning to do, you have an ethical duty to prevent this. All counsellors have both a 'duty of care' and a duty to prevent harm whenever possible. Before you act on any concern of this kind there are a couple of important things to do:

1 Inquire more of your client what she has in mind and get as full a picture as possible.

2 Talk straightaway to your supervisor to check out your thinking and get a second opinion.

If when you have taken both these steps you are sure your original thinking is accurate, you should tell your client of your concerns in a way that is therapeutically sensitive and work with her to look at how mishaps can be avoided. On the other hand, if you have any doubts remaining you should first clarify them before deciding on the most appropriate course of action.

Case example: Angie

Angie's decision

Angie saw her counsellor a few days after her return from Manchester. She was in high spirits. She thought her interview had gone reasonably well, although there were a few things she wished she had done differently. But by and large she had felt confident and in charge of the situation. The next step would involve her in a full day of different kinds of tests. If she were successful she would be sent on a two-week training course, prior to commencing her new post.

Angie felt she needed to do some intense preparation for the day of tests and wanted to free up as much time as possible. She told her counsellor she would like to miss her next appointment and come again once she had completed the tests.

Her counsellor's reaction

Angie's counsellor had to suppress her immediate desire to disagree. Privately she thought this was the wrong moment to be cutting down on sessions. She felt the support Angie would gain would counterbalance her need for time. She felt worried. If Angie moved too fast into independence it could cause her to falter. She might even fluff the test day.

A number of 'compromises' went through her mind. She could suggest Angie kept in touch by phone. Angie could come in for half a session so that she kept in touch but gained time. She could suggest meeting at a different time that fitted in better with Angie's plans.

Each time she thought of a solution she rejected it because she recognized she was trying to solve a problem that did not exist for her client. She was trying to meet her own needs and soothe her own worries. Angie had made a decision that needed accepting unequivocally. Whatever happened, no serious harm was likely to result from missing one session. There was no ethical dilemma here. And soon the day would come when Angie would be making all her decisions without her counsellor knowing anything about it. She had to step back, allow Angie to make her own decisions and give her unreserved support.

The next session

Angie came to her next session in a slightly subdued frame of mind. She got herself into a state of high anxiety in preparing for the tests and thought she hadn't done as well as she could. She thought she might have failed.

Her counsellor felt a momentary guilt pang. She should have stepped in, said something. She could have prevented this. But then she caught herself. She reminded herself that the whole point of this phase of the work was to support autonomous choice and that problems like this were bound to occur. Her task was to help Angie figure out where she had gone off course and how to prevent this in the future.

The result

As it turned out, Angie had in fact passed the test with flying colours and was offered the post. She was, of course, thrilled. But she also learned a lot about herself and her inclination to easily feel 'down' when she felt she hadn't given of her best. She decided she wanted to learn how to keep herself on more of an even keel at such times because with a number of important challenges ahead she would need the ability to do this.

Her counsellor agreed that this would be very valuable, and so the last stage of the contract was put in place as the end of Angie's counselling moved ever closer.

Key skills

The skills required of the counsellor at this stage are to:

◆ always support autonomous choice
◆ reassure when needed
◆ suppress helpful responses
◆ avoid an 'I saw this coming' reaction.

Summary

You and your client have now completed your therapeutic contract. The difficulties that brought your client to you are now resolved. Your client is ready to take their last step with you – ending and saying 'goodbye' – as they continue along their life's path without you. In the next chapter we will focus on how to make that ending.

Key concepts used are:

◆ autonomy

◆ synthesis and integration.

Key skills include:

◆ constancy

◆ encouragement

◆ positive stroking

◆ explanation

◆ answering questions directly

◆ answering questions indirectly

◆ contract review.

Exercises

Select a client with whom you have finished working and think back to the point when your client was making the transition into autonomy. Listen to an audiotape of the session, if you have one, and carry out the following:

9.1 Review your use of skills:
  ◆ What were the key areas of synthesis and integration?
  ◆ What issues generated excitement?
  ◆ What issues generated despondency?
  ◆ What questions did your client ask?
  ◆ Which ones did you answer directly? What was your thinking in answering in this way? How did your client respond to your answers?
  ◆ Which ones did you answer indirectly? What was your thinking in answering in this way? How did your client respond to your answers?
  ◆ What approach did you take to contract review?
  ◆ What was the contract you agreed?
  ◆ Was it successful?
  ◆ What anxieties did your client express?
  ◆ How did you work with them?
9.2 Review your interpersonal approach:
  ◆ Review your strengths and weaknesses in offering support from the sidelines.
  ◆ What personal qualities did you bring to the relationship that encouraged your client to learn from her errors?
  ◆ What personal qualities did you bring to the relationship that inhibited your client in learning from her errors?
  ◆ What were the biggest challenges for you in working through this phase with your client?
  ◆ How did you use supervisory help?
9.3 Check through all your answers. Identify your strengths and areas for development.
9.4 Make a plan to meet your learning needs.

Notes

1   'The patient stabilizes his or her redecisions, recognizing and accepting in the here-and-now the separation between his or her own self and that of the therapist. In this phase the patient's level of autonomy is analysed by exploring the amount of awareness, spontaneity, and intimacy expressed by the patient with the therapist': M. Novellino and C. Moiso, 'The psychodynamic approach to transactional analysis', *Transactional Analysis Journal*, 20, 3 (1990), p. 190.

2   'The Decisive Intervention, which is the introduction of new messages (usually Permissions) into the patient's Parent ego state, allows the Adult to take over from the Script Parent, so that the Natural Child may be freed. This is called "flipping out of the script and flipping into the real world", the striking of the old show and putting a new show on the road': S. Swede, *How To Cure: How Eric Berne Practised Transactional Analysis* (Boyce, Corte Mader, CA, 1977), p. 4.

3   E. Berne, *Games People Play* (Penguin, Harmondsworth, 1964/1985), p. 16.

4   'In this . . . phase, that of *rapprochement*, while individuation proceeds very rapidly and the Child exercises it to the limit, he also becomes more and more aware of his separateness . . . one cannot emphasize too strongly the importance of . . . optimal emotional availability': M. Mahler, F. Pine and A. Bergman, *The Psychological Birth of the Human Infant* (Maresfield, London, 1989), pp. 77, 78.

5   Swede, *How To Cure*, p. 4.

Further reading

Berne, E. (1964/1985) *Games People Play*. Harmondsworth: Penguin. Chapter 17.
Stewart, I. (1992) *Eric Berne*. London: Sage. Chapter 3, pp. 82–5.

10 · Ending and Separating

The aim of this phase is to facilitate an ending. The expected outcomes are:

◆ to prepare to let go of the client

◆ to create a structure for ending

◆ to implement and monitor the progress of the ending

◆ to say a final 'goodbye'.

Counsellors are continuously making and ending relationships. The frequency with which this happens is entirely dependent on the structure of your practice.

Short-term work

Over the last decade the demand for counselling has dramatically risen, particularly in primary care and through employee assistance programmes. Counsellors are increasingly expected to undertake short-term work, commonly of between four and six sessions. Where such demands are placed on counsellors the bottom line is usually an economic one of funding. There is simply not the money available to provide more. It is beyond the scope of this book to look at the issues behind such decisions, or indeed the rightness of the decisions themselves. Suffice to say there are cogent arguments on both sides of the debate. What we do need to consider is the impact on the counsellor of ending with a continuous stream of clients every four to six weeks. The toll is enormous. Counsellors I have spoken to use words like 'conveyor belt' and 'burned out' to describe the way they feel about a working week based on a predominantly short-term caseload. Making and ending meaningful relationships at this pace requires enormous emotional stamina and a great capacity for self-maintenance. There is an obvious danger that the counsellor, in order to protect herself, simply ceases to give of her best and relies on mechanistic approaches that are less demanding. In terms of ending with a client this might result in

◆ simply going through the motions of making a 'good' ending

◆ feeling relief that yet another client has finished

◆ ignoring the fact that an ending is taking place.

Sometimes, of course, the converse happens and a client walks into your consulting room who makes an emotional impact on you. They touch you deeply: the pain of their dilemma, the pathos of their situation, cut you to the quick. They need so much more than you can offer; you want to offer it, but you know you can't. You do not lack the skill or the willingness, but your service is short term and you are powerless to alter this.

What can counsellors do to protect themselves from these kinds of stresses? There are a number of things that can take away some of the strain.

♦ Wherever possible, diversify your practice by working with both short- and longer-term contracts. This may mean establishing a range of practice settings.

♦ Work in a variety of ways, for example with individuals, with couples, and with time-limited groups based on a specific issue such as anger management.

♦ Become skilled at self-maintenance. Ensure you have rich and varied sources of strokes that keep you feeling 'topped up'.

♦ Combat 'counsellor isolation' by ensuring you are part of supportive peer groups in your place of work, if this is possible. If it isn't, find external peer support groups.

♦ Use supervision in a way that is restorative.

What is there on the positive side?

In short-term work, clients are more likely to return for another set of sessions. Re-establishing a relationship is normally easier than starting a new one and can often be a source of pleasure. So you can look forward to saying 'hello' again to some of the clients you say 'goodbye' to.

Building your skills in long-term work can be very satisfying and TA is particularly well suited to being adapted to short-term work. Sharing the TA model with clients enables them to go away with a useful tool, which they use in times of stress and difficulty. A little help can go a long way, and one of the pleasures of short-term work is witnessing the big changes some clients make in just a few sessions. Truly this is a case of 'less is more'.

Longer-term work

An absolute 'goodbye'

'Goodbye' for counsellors doing longer-term work usually means making an absolute ending. Saying goodbye to clients with whom you have worked closely over an extended period can be emotionally demanding. In most cases you are unlikely to meet the person again. Some clients may send you the occasional card to let you know a piece of news or to mark Christmas or other significant times, and occasionally a client may return to do a follow-up piece of work. But, generally, these are infrequent occurrences.

Letting go of involvement

For the counselling relationship to be effective, a real bond will have been established between you and your client. This bond is based on real feelings on both sides. Inevitably, the longer you work with someone the stronger your feelings are likely to be. Although we know when we establish the initial contract that saying goodbye is the end we are working towards, we are also human beings with human feelings and human needs, and letting go can raise a range of emotions in us. Making a relationship with our client involves being interested in their life, caring about them, wanting them to achieve the best that they can. And although as counsellors we don't actually become involved in our client's life, generally we feel highly involved. Indeed, it is this feeling of involvement on which our bond with our client is based; without it we could not be effective. In finishing a piece of counselling one of the principal tasks for the counsellor is to prepare herself to relinquish her involvement – to be able to accept that the work is over and that the time when you will no longer be needed is close at hand. Your job is done. Your usefulness is nearly at an end, your role obsolete. Your client will move ahead without you and you will no longer know what takes place in her life. No matter how pleased you are for your client that she has reached this point – or, as is sometimes the case, relieved that your client is leaving – you are still experiencing a loss and will need to grieve for this.

How do I let go?

Preparing yourself to be in a place, personally, where you can say goodbye with good grace and without any undermining reluctance lurking, involves several important steps that you may do alone, through self-supervision, or with your supervisor. The following are key.

An overall assessment of the work

- ◆ Reviewing and reflecting on all stages of the counselling, in particular, recalling the client's starting point and the staging posts along the way.

- ◆ Recalling what you liked best about your own work and giving yourself positive strokes for it.

◆ Letting yourself know your errors and weak points, focusing on how you tried to correct these.

◆ Being candid with yourself about how successful you were. What is the learning in this for you?

Recognizing what the client means for you

◆ Taking note of your aspirations for your client and looking at what it would mean to you for your client to achieve them.

◆ Taking note of your greatest disappointment and your greatest pleasure in your client.

◆ Asking yourself what aspect of you is most invested in the relationship and why.

◆ Accounting for the kinds of strokes you derive from the relationship.

◆ Focusing on what you will find most difficult to let go of and why.

Looking at endings in your own life

◆ Your general pattern in making endings.

◆ Your strengths in making endings and how you can take these into the work with your client.

◆ Your vulnerabilities in making endings and how you will protect you and your client from these.

Looking at how your client makes endings and any links this might have with you

◆ Explore significant endings your clients have made in the past.

◆ Is there a pattern?

◆ Is this pattern recurring?

Case example: Angie
The counsellor's preparation for letting go

Her overall assessment of the work

As she reviewed her work, Angie's counsellor recalled the anxious, highly distressed young woman whom she had first met. She remembered how caught up Angie, or Angela, as she called herself then, had been with her family – how she had felt unable to strike out in her own direction for fear of failing her parents.

She recalled the slow painstaking work when often there seemed little change in Angie; the growth of Angie's self-confidence, as the work with her Parent and Child ego states gradually freed her Adult and allowed it to emerge; the moment of breakthrough when Angie finally dared show her anger; the shortening of her name and the creating of her own Adult identity, no longer the pleasing child, but a grown woman with a mature identity; and now, branching out in a whole new direction.

What Angie's counsellor most liked about her own work was her ability to use a slow patient style that didn't frighten Angie's Child or alienate her Parent. In hindsight, she had effectively matched her approach to what her client could tolerate at every step. This had been the bedrock on which the success of the work had been built.

The counsellor thought her weak spot in working with Angie had been a tendency towards symbiosis with her. On reflection, she didn't feel this had undermined the work in any serious way, but she had come too close for comfort on a number of occasions. She decided to look at this issue in supervision to assess whether it was a general weakness in her work or whether it was something specific in the process with Angie. But, overall, she thought the work with Angie had been successful.

Recognizing Angie's significance

Angie's counsellor had already recognized the high yield of positive strokes she received from working with her client. She knew that her work with Angie enhanced her self-esteem and made her feel good. Nobody would want to let go of such richness. But she had by now come to terms with the loss. She could boost her self-esteem in other ways – through work with other clients or through other forms of professional activity such as a conference presentation that could bring additional strokes from colleagues.

Her biggest aspiration for Angie was that she would establish herself in a lifestyle that she felt matched her real wants and needs – that her counselling would have set her free to find the path to her goal. Immediately she identified this, she recognized how her own esteem might become intertwined with such a hope. It would be important to focus with Angie on her own aspirations for herself.

Angie's counsellor felt very little disappointment in her client. When she realized this she was quite surprised. Her guess would have been that something would disappoint her keenly, that this part of Angie's script story would somehow be replayed in the counselling. That it wasn't was a positive indication that her script really had been changed. On reflection this was her greatest pleasure.

Angie's counsellor knew she had a particular investment in young people setting out on their life path. When she, herself, had been young a family friend had helped her at a critical moment, preventing her from failing her degree. Often, the right kind of help at the right moment meant a young person could make really significant changes that impacted their life course. She found this a particular source of satisfaction. Not knowing whether Angie's future progress would be hard, she took real pleasure in Angie's development. She knew she would have to let go.

Endings in the counsellor's own life

Angie's counsellor had no patterns of any significance with regard to endings. She was generally effective and sensitive in the way she worked with her clients in this phase. She knew, however, she had become particularly fond of Angie, largely because of her youthfulness, and that this would be the issue to be alert to. She would need to be in a place where she could use her affection as the springboard from which to be wholeheartedly willing to let go and guard against any symbiotic invitation to Angie to carry on as a way of receiving positive strokes for herself.

Every counsellor has their own way of preparing for the ending. Angie's counsellor liked to take a walk in the woods and remind herself that the natural beauty she enjoyed so much was dependent on seasonal cycles; these involved a time of letting go. As she walked she made a mental image of Angie. She pictured her confident and excited and felt joy in her client's accomplishments. How could she want to hold on? To hold on would be to stultify and to confine Angie's essential life force. It would be like trying to make a beautiful young tree grow in the shade of another. It would be an act of selfishness. As she accepted the truth of her own reflections she felt ready to let Angie go. She had found the healer in herself. As a healer, she was the custodian of the counselling journey, responsible for ensuring a safe arrival at the agreed destination. She had no ownership rights over either the client or her journey. Angie's counsellor knew she could now facilitate her client's leaving in a spirit of generosity and good will.

Key skills

The skills required of the counsellor in this process are:

♦ making an overall assessment of the work
♦ recognizing what the client means to you
♦ looking at endings in your own life
♦ finding the healer in you that wants to let go.

Structuring the final phase

Creating the right structure for the ending phase is very important. It is a key part of providing security, consistency and predictability, essential prerequisites that allow your client to focus on completing her work.

There are a number of things to consider in creating a structure for the ending phase.

Planning the ending date

It is important to decide together on an ending date. This gives reality to the ending for both you and your client and allows each of you the opportunity to say what you feel is right for the circumstances.

The date you decide on should allow time for completion of your final contract, as well as a chance to reflect on the work you have done together and to say goodbye to each other.

Although there are no hard and fast rules about setting the ending date, there are some pitfalls to be avoided such as:

◆ setting a premature date because either you or your client wants to hurry things along

◆ setting a date that is too far ahead as a way of trying to hold on and put off the end.

To underline the importance of making time and space for ending, many counsellors write into the administrative contract a specified minimum number of sessions that will be dedicated to ending.

The right frequency of sessions

You and your client will need to discuss what is now the right frequency of sessions. She may spontaneously raise it with you, but if she doesn't you will need to.

Questions to discuss are:

◆ Do you want to continue at the usual frequency? If so, why is this helpful?

◆ Is it a good idea to look at a point when you might decrease the frequency of your sessions as part of helping your client adjust to letting go?

◆ Is a pattern of incrementally decreasing over time right – such as going from weekly, to fortnightly, to monthly sessions?

◆ Is decreasing the frequency incrementally too protracted? Is a sharper focus needed, such as four more sessions at fortnightly intervals and then stop?

◆ Would a follow-up session be helpful?

Planning how to end

Discussion of the ending should also focus on how this will be done. Clients commonly have clear preferences about how they want to say goodbye and the rituals that are important to them in doing this. Rituals mark a rite of passage. Ending a period of personal counselling is an important milestone to mark.

Some of the rituals my own clients have found important include:

- having a cup of tea and a piece of cake together in the last session

- planting a rose bush as a way of symbolizing that personal growth and development will continue beyond the counselling work

- for a client who had been bereaved, bringing a photograph of a much loved partner and 'talking to her' about how he was now ready to look for a new partner and pick up his life whilst still cherishing her memory and the years they had shared together.

Case example: Angie

Angie set a date for ending that was just a few sessions ahead. Having already changed to fortnightly sessions she had established a frequency with which she was comfortable. Incrementally decreasing the frequency of her sessions any further was unnecessary and would be more likely to support script rather than autonomy. Angie needed a sharply focused ending to fit with the changes she had made.

In looking at how she wanted to end, Angie decided she would like to spend one of her last sessions making a collage of pictures and words to symbolize the things she wanted to create in the next chapter of her life. By sharing her hopes and dreams with her counsellor in this way she would be building an emotional bridge between her present, in which her counsellor had an important place, and her future that would not include the counsellor. She would take with her the permission to pursue her goals. If, in the early stages of the next phase, she faltered momentarily or came up against difficulties, she would be able to draw on her memory of making the collage in session as additional support and encouragement.

Key skills

The skills required of the counsellor here are:

- Agree an end date.
- Check the date will neither protract nor curtail the work.

- ◆ Agree the frequency of sessions.
- ◆ Discuss how your client wants to end.
- ◆ Discuss any ending rituals that are important to your client.

Planning, implementing and monitoring the work

There are a number of important areas to focus on as you plan and implement the end of your work with your client.

Checking completion of the contract

As your client moves towards an end you need to run some checks to satisfy yourself that the contract has been met:

- ◆ Does your client feel satisfied with her changes or does she perceive gaps?

- ◆ Is your client generally thinking, feeling and behaving in ways that are congruent with successful contract completion?

- ◆ Does your client report other people noticing changes in her?

- ◆ Does your client feel that the gap left by giving up script ways is now fully met by her new autonomous lifestyle?

- ◆ Has she moved beyond any grief for her former script-bound self into pleasure in her new autonomous self?

- ◆ Do both you and your client agree on the outcomes that have been achieved?

Going through the areas suggested should alert you to any problems that need resolving in order to ensure a satisfactory conclusion and give you a clear idea of any issues which need attention.

Failure in the counselling as the reason for an incomplete contract

From time to time, all counsellors find that an ending is being planned because the counselling is not proving satisfactory. The reasons why a piece of counselling fails can be many. Some of the most common ones are:

- ◆ There is a mismatch between your client's expectations and the reality of what you can offer.

- ◆ The counsellor wants more for the client than the client wants for herself.

- ◆ The approach you offer does not meet the client's needs.

- ◆ There is antipathy in the relationship between you that is irreconcilable.

- ◆ An error you have made has proven impossible to put right.

- ◆ Your client had an ulterior motive in seeking counselling, for example wanting to 'look good' in someone else's eyes. This need has now abated and your client feels no desire to continue.

- ◆ A game has been played out between you that supports your client's and/or your own script.

Example

Elaine was ready to end her counselling and at the same time was coming to the end of a university access course which she had embarked on with the support of her counsellor. In the penultimate session Elaine said that she had enjoyed the access course but had decided that university was not for her and that she would explore other employment options. Secretly disappointed, her counsellor suggested to Elaine that it was a great pity to waste such a valuable opportunity to 'get on in life'. Elaine was taken aback; she felt devalued and undermined. Although she talked this through with her counsellor, nevertheless, she ended feeling that somehow she was not good enough and had been a disappointment to her counsellor.

In supervision, the counsellor identified that she had played out a game with her client. From a misguided desire to help the client 'better herself' (strong messages in her own script) she had attempted to 'rescue' the client by encouraging her to go on to a full-time degree course. Moving to the 'victim' position, the client felt 'persecuted' by the counsellor. The counsellor realized that she had projected her own aspirations onto the client and her own desires for the 'perfect' client. The counsellor moved into her own script and reinforced the client's script as a way of avoiding her own feelings about the ending.

Where the decision to end is based on something problematic, your first step must be to seek supervision in order to invite someone who is outside the process between you and your client to give you their perspective and support. Then you need to make a plan to bring the counselling to the best ending that is possible in the circumstances. If the ending is taking place early on in the work it is generally easier to make a 'good enough' ending than if you are far on in the counselling when this is usually more complex.

What to do in situations of therapeutic error

If you have made errors, including playing out a game, or if there is irreconcilable antipathy, what does good professional practice suggest is needed to make the best outcome possible? Codes of ethics and professional practice offer helpful guiding principles. But also ask yourself, 'What would I expect of my counsellor if I were in my client's shoes?' In circumstances like these, counsellors sometimes become afraid of the client for several reasons and worry that the client will:

♦ not come back

♦ get angry and make a 'bad' ending

♦ tarnish their professional reputation

♦ bring a formal complaint.

Unintentionally, the counsellor may start to disengage from their client as a self-protective strategy. A focus on your own self-protection usually gives rise to a defensive attitude, which generally results in defensive practice. The focus on what is best for the client becomes lost. The golden rule is never allow your fears to dominate you. Fear inhibits clear thinking.

♦ Always discuss possible therapeutic errors in supervision. Even if you feel some shame, don't hide.

♦ Talk your anxieties through with your supervisor and look at whether there is a reality base to them.

♦ Look at whether or not you are in fact feeling something that belongs with your client that she is excluding.

♦ Discuss appropriate strategies and approaches with your supervisor.

♦ Mentally discipline yourself to return to your client with an open, contactful and non-defensive attitude, believing both of you are 'OK'.

♦ Remember to apologize for your mistakes. Counsellors are human and make mistakes. Accepting this and being prepared to apologize will go a long way in repairing a rupture in the therapeutic relationship.

Following these guidelines will create optimal conditions for making the best possible ending.

In formulating your counselling plans also consider whether or not there is a need for your client to be referred on to another colleague. If there is, do you have someone in mind who would be right, or do you need to direct your client to someone else who would be able to help find another counsellor?

Example

Judith left a message on her counsellor's answering machine cancelling her next appointment and making it clear that she did not want to rebook. Her counsellor knew the reason immediately. She had made a therapeutic error in the last session by confronting some of Judith's actions rather than retaining her empathic stance. Her client felt understandably wounded and mistreated. Judith was extremely sensitive and confrontation had never been an appropriate response to her. Her counsellor had found something Judith said about the future of her marriage so alarming that she had made an unconsidered response on the spur of the moment.

The counsellor telephoned her client immediately. Judith was icy cold and could not be persuaded to come along to discuss things.

In supervision the counsellor explored her error and its results. She was both worried and scared. She felt worried about her client's well-being. It was not good to leave a client high and dry in the middle of an important piece of work. But she was also scared because Judith had several times expressed vengeful thoughts as she talked about her life. Might she feel these feelings towards her counsellor? If she did, what might she do?

Her supervisor helped her to explore her fears. The reality was she had made an error and there was a possibility that the client might wish to make a complaint. Her supervisor reminded her that this is a daily reality for all counsellors and something that all counsellors had to come to terms with.

Her supervisor encouraged her to refocus on the client and to look at what she might need even if she gave the appearance of rejecting it. Showing sensitivity to Judith was the best she could offer and might soothe some of her distress. It also provided the best possibility of stemming any negative reactions.

The counsellor decided to write to her client acknowledging that Judith had probably felt hurt by the last session. In her letter she included a bull's-eye transaction that was intended to speak to Judith on all levels. The counsellor reiterated her suggestion that she and her client meet for a session to discuss the issue and to look at the way forward for Judith.

It was some weeks before Judith responded. Although reluctant, she was willing to come for a meeting to discuss what had happened. During the session the counsellor focused on the way she had failed to meet Judith with empathy and understanding. Judith was moved by the counsellor's willingness to own her mistakes and accepted her apology. However, she was unwilling to continue and wished to end.

Although she managed some repair of the rupture to the relationship, the counsellor is still coming to terms with the effects of her error and the very unsatisfactory loose ends it has left for everyone.

The client does not reach script cure

Many clients do not attain complete script change, and counselling ends with the acknowledgement that the best that is possible in the circumstances has been achieved. Increasingly, many TA counsellors would see non-script cure as the more likely and more realistic outcome in most instances. This is partly because script cure normally takes a long time to achieve and many counsellors do not offer the length of contract that it requires. But the view is also growing that script cure may, in many cases, be an unrealistic goal and that the concept itself needs reviewing.

When script cure has been unsuccessfully aimed for, it is important for the counsellor to analyse the reasons. Some useful questions to ask are:

◆ Was the goal unrealistic?

◆ Was the goal within the limits of my competence?

◆ Did the client have insufficient resources to attain the goals, e.g. did they have enough external support?

◆ Would my colleagues think script cure is attainable with this kind of script issue?

◆ If script cure were attainable, what would be needed to make it possible?

Having found some preliminary answers, you can now follow them to track the reasons to a more solid conclusion. From there you can plan how to end the counselling most appropriately.

What is absolutely vital is that we have a 'good enough' script change. From the client's point of view they have achieved satisfaction in the counselling process and a reasonable resolution to their difficulties. To over-invest in change is to get caught up in the drive to be perfect and is undermining for the client as well as the counsellor.

Example

Kevin sought counselling because of his depression. As his symptoms abated he began to glimpse the root of the problem. At 54 he was no longer as charismatic as he had once been. In both his personal and his professional life he felt he was 'losing his touch'. Kevin wanted to 'be the man I used to be.' He would spend a lot of each session recounting an impressive list of 'successes' he had achieved. Clearly, he wanted reinforcing positive strokes for these in order to support his flagging self-esteem.

It became clear that Kevin's past 'success' was based on a combination of factors that it would be hard for him to regain: a youthful, athletic physique, a 'high-flyer' persona and a large income that had dried up since he had taken voluntary redundancy. Kevin had used the lump sum from his redundancy to start a business venture that had failed. Financially, things were tight.

Kevin's counsellor began to realize that the original contract to 'feel good about myself again' was based on Kevin's belief he could recapture his former self. Sadly, his self-esteem had been built on thin ice – money, good looks and charm. These were external props, not internal strengths. Now he was faced with trying to regain self-esteem without these props. He would probably never feel as 'good' about himself as he had done in the past. The counsellor's task was to help him find a way to feel 'good enough' about himself as he rebuilt a life based on the reality of what he could achieve. The contract agreed originally could not be completed because it was based on unrealistic expectations. It would have to be reviewed and renegotiated. This would be a delicate process in which Kevin's sensitivity to feeling shamed and humiliated must be protected. Script cure was an inappropriate and unrealistic goal for Kevin. It would be important to protect him from feeling a failure because of the change in goal that was needed.

Reviewing and reminiscing

At the end of a longer-term piece of counselling it is easy to forget how things were in the beginning. An important part of ending is recalling the starting point so that your client fully accounts to herself for the changes she has made. It is easy to diminish or overlook changes because, once they have been made and incorporated in daily life, they become the norm and it can be hard to remember 'what I was like before'. Reviewing the work offers your client the opportunity to reflect on her achievements and to take pleasure in the changes she has made.

Key skills

When reviewing, remember to ask your client:

- To identify the peak moments that stand out as significant, both positive and negative.
- To share moments that have made her laugh.
- To reflect on what she finds most significant about her change.
- To reflect on her relationship with you. What has it been like? Did you surprise her? What did she find most helpful? What was least helpful? Is there anything you could have done differently?
- To talk about what she will miss most and what she will miss least.

Reminisce with your client about her journey:

◆ Sharing your involvement along the way and some of the key positive moments for you.
◆ Stroke her and validate her change.
◆ Share what you will miss about seeing her so that she can leave feeling you care about her going and that she has made an impact on you.

Case example: Angie

There were several key moments for Angie. Expressing her anger for the first time was one of the most significant. Equally significant was something that her counsellor barely remembered, a time when Angie had been very upset towards the end of a session and she had extended the session time by a few minutes to give her an opportunity to finish what she needed to say.

Angie: I know that it was really inconvenient for you. That was when I knew you really cared and that I could trust you.

Like many counsellors, Angie's reflected yet again that no matter what she thought were key interventions, it is often the case that your client is impacted by something you may not recall and certainly wasn't in your counselling plan! It really is the quality of the relationship that matters most. Technical skills are, of course, important but they take second place to the quality of relationship.

On the negative side, Angie had been offended when her counsellor asked if she felt the need of a locum during a longish holiday period.

Angie: I felt you didn't trust me to take care of myself. Like you were offering me a babysitter.

As with impactful positive actions, those that the client finds unhelpful or unacceptable are often quite a surprise and may include things that are considered good practice. Angie's counsellor reflected that often clients don't say how they feel at the time, which is why it is so important to give them an opportunity to do so before they leave.

Angie continued:

Angie: The worst moment was when I knew I had gone too far to go back and I couldn't see a way forward. I felt desperate, like I had made a big mistake by not stopping earlier when everything was going so well. I hope I never feel like that again.

Angie's experience is one shared by many clients who undertake longer-term work. The feeling of relief and positivity that comes from the early stages disappears when deeper layers of script are worked with. It can seem an eternity before a feeling of well-being returns.

Angie said she would miss the feeling of safety that came from knowing her counsellor was there if she needed her:

Angie: What I won't miss is the battling with myself! It will be nice to leave some of the struggles behind.

Angie's counsellor stroked her for her commitment and tenacity as well as the changes she had made. She told Angie how much she had enjoyed working with her and that she would miss knowing about the developments in her life. She recalled a number of key moments in the counselling when the strength of Angie's determination had touched her. Angie's expression showed clearly how important it was to her to hear things from her counsellor's perspective.

Gifts

To accept gifts or not always poses an ethical dilemma. On the one hand you don't want to offend the client by rejecting a genuine expression of thanks, but on the other accepting a gift may reinforce symbiosis and script. A gift may be a way of clients leaving a part of themselves with you. You have to judge what they may be seeking to leave and whether this is a good idea. The easiest way to manage the issue of gifts is to establish your own policy and clarify it at the outset.

A no-gifts policy
This is a straightforward policy to establish and maintain.

Example

Steve knew his counsellor shared a love of the same kind of music as he did. In his last session he brought out a tape he had compiled of his own favourite music.

Steve: I made this tape for you from my own library.

His counsellor took the tape and studied the titles of the songs Steve had recorded.

Counsellor: You've chosen some wonderful stuff. I'm really touched by your thoughtfulness. But as I explained at the start of our work together, I don't accept gifts.

His counsellor then handed the tape back. At first, Steve looked surprised and slightly wounded. But then his expression changed.

Steve: I'd forgotten. Oh! well, I suppose I can always play it in the car.
Counsellor: That would be a great place to enjoy such classic tracks.

Steve's counsellor is sensitive in the way he says 'no'. He takes the tape and reads the cover, stroking his client for his choice of tracks. He acknowledges Steve and the intention behind the gift. Steve is not humiliated or rejected. Only the tape is rejected.

An open policy

This is the most complex policy to manage because you have to be able to justify saying 'yes' to some clients and 'no' to others. There is also the possibility that two or more of your clients may know each other. If they compare notes and find you accepted a gift from one of them but not the other, they may draw inaccurate conclusions about your reasons that are potentially damaging to both of them. To practise this approach you need very clear therapeutic reasons to justify your decision and a clear way of implementing it.

An accepting gifts policy

Many counsellors do accept gifts from their clients. If you wish to do this you need to think through some of the following areas:

- What is my therapeutic justification for doing this?
- How is it in my client's best interest?
- What will I do with the gift?
- What evidence do I have that shows I am not reinforcing my client's script?
- If I were challenged, how would I demonstrate that I was not exploiting my client?
- Do I have any limits on the kinds of gifts I accept? For example, would I differentiate between accepting a small trinket and a case of wine? If I would, why would I? How would I explain this to a client?
- If you make no differentiation about the kinds of gifts you accept, what difficulties could this raise for you and your clients?
- Are there any ethical issues to consider?

Unless you practise a no-gifts policy, the issue is complex and needs careful thought.

Boundaries

It is not unusual for a client to harbour the hope that at the end of counselling the boundaries of the relationship can be changed and put on a social footing. The desire to be 'friends' to 'meet for coffee' or even 'to get to know one another better', with all its ulterior significance, indicates a desire to continue the relationship and an unwillingness to let go. Clients express this hope in a variety of ways that can range from the charming, 'You must have such interesting ideas on life', to the angry, 'You don't really care about me. I'm just your 10 o'clock appointment.'

If your client expresses a desire to shift the counselling boundary:

◆ Make it clear that this is not in her best interest, no matter how much she believes it to be, and that you can be of greatest help to her by staying firmly focused on her needs. The contract was established with an understanding that your wants, needs and feelings were not part of the relationship. The space is hers. To alter this would be to do her a serious disservice.

◆ Focus on the underlying reluctance to let go and help your client to resolve it.

◆ Restate the ethical position of the professional relationship.

Contact after the end of counselling

Sometimes, clients will ask you whether they can return if they ever feel the need. You have to decide whether this question stems from normal anxiety about the impending ending, a reluctance to say goodbye, or the fact that something is incomplete in the work. Your response will vary according to what you identify as the source of the question.

Most TA counsellors would accept a client back to do further work where the need arises. For example, one client retuned to his counsellor after a five-year gap when he was diagnosed with a life threatening illness. He wanted help and support from someone who knew him well and whom he trusted as he faced a testing time.

If you indicate a willingness to be available to a client in the future, be sure this is not symbiotically reinforcing. And always make it clear that if, at some point in the future, your client identifies a need for further help, you would also be willing to help her find another counsellor to work with if she wanted to do so. This helps stem any symbiotic dynamic and shows your client your openness to her moving beyond you to someone else.

The second 'big' question about further contact is, 'Can I write to you, e-mail you, telephone you?' Again this needs careful thinking through for the reasons already given. Most TA counsellors are happy to hear from former clients on an infrequent basis. For example, one of my clients wrote to tell me that she had given birth to her first child after years of unsuccessfully trying to become pregnant.

Do make sure your client doesn't see any future communication as a way to continue their relationship with you by post. And make sure you do not raise any expectations that you will write back. Even if in the event you decide a brief note back is a good idea, you need to create in the client the expectation that they will not hear from you. Otherwise you could find yourself manipulated into entering into a relationship by correspondence, or creating feelings of rejection in your client because you have not replied.

The final session

And so you reach the final session. What are the areas to be aware of?

◆ Be vigilant about any subtle invitations from your client to reinforce script. Many clients unawarely have one last attempt at trying to undermine themselves by prompting you into a gallows transaction with them or some other form of self-sabotage. Be on your mettle from the moment you meet your client until the door has closed behind her.

◆ Stay in role; don't use the last session as an opportunity to relax your professionalism. For example, if you have not used touch, don't suddenly use it in the last session. Stay consistent, predictable and professional.

◆ Listen to the last three minutes with as much attention as the first three of the first session. They provide a summary of the outcome of the work from your client's viewpoint.

◆ In particular, focus on the final transaction between you and your client. It is the final seal on the work and contains in miniature what you have achieved together.

◆ Allow yourself some time after the session to gather your thoughts. It has been a 'big' session for you, too. You need some reflective space.

Making a good ending is a skilled job. It demands careful thought and sensitive implementation. You need the capacity to stay in relationship whilst letting go; the wisdom to know when the end has been reached; and the integrity to let go in the best way possible.

> No man can reveal to you aught but that which already lies half asleep in the dawning of your knowledge . . . If he is indeed wise he does not bid you enter the house of his wisdom, but rather leads you to the threshold of your own mind.[1]

Summary

And so your client has ended and the work you have done is complete. Of course, this does not mean you will stop thinking about her. For every counsellor there is a period of reflection that comes in the wake of completion.

Some important questions to ponder are:

◆ How was I most effective?

◆ Where was I least effective? Why?

◆ What have I learned as a counsellor from working with this client?

◆ How can I further develop my therapeutic skills?

Key concepts in ending are:

◆ contract review

◆ strokes

◆ rituals

◆ ulterior transactions

◆ gallows transaction.

Key skills include:

◆ self-reflection

◆ letting go

◆ planning

◆ initiating supervisory consultation.

Exercise

10.1 With a partner:

(a) Identify whether your own practice is of predominantly short- or long-term work and the kinds of pressures this brings for making endings.

(b) How do you normally manage these pressures? Are you happy about your approach? Are there any changes you want to make?

(c) Focus on endings in your own life and consider:
   - your general pattern in making endings
   - your strengths in making endings and how you can take these into the work with your client
   - your vulnerabilities in making endings and how you will protect yourself and your client from these.

(d) Where an ending came about because of an error you had made, how would you be likely to respond? What strengths and vulnerabilities does your response indicate?

(e) Discuss your approach to gifts and how effective you find it.

(f) How do you manage situations where a client wants to change the boundaries of the relationship?

Notes

1   Kahlil Gibran, *The Prophet* (Heinemann, London, 1969), p. 67.

References

Berne, E. (1961) *Transactional Analysis in Psychotherapy*. New York: Grove Press.

Berne, E. (1964/85) *Games People Play*. Harmondsworth, Middlesex: Penguin Books.

Berne, E. (1966/78) *Principles of Group Treatment*. New York: Grove Press.

Berne, E. (1970/81) *Sex In Human Loving*. Harmondsworth, Middlesex: Penguin Books.

Berne, E. (1972/87) *What Do You Say After You Say Hello?* London: Corgi Books.

Clarkson, P. & Fish, S. (1988) 'Rechilding: Creating a New Past in the Present as a Support for the Future', *Transactional Analysis Journal*, Vol. 18 (1).

Clarkson, P. & Gilbert, M. (1988) 'Berne's Original Model of Ego States: Some Theoretical Considerations', *Transactional Analysis Journal*,. Vol. 18 (1), pp. 20–29.

Dashiell, S. R. (1978) 'The Parent Resolution Process: Reprogramming Psychic Incorporations in the Parent', *Transactional Analysis Journal*, Vol. 10 (4).

English, F. (1972) 'Sleepy, Spunky And Spooky: A Revised Second Order Structural Diagram And Script Matrix', *Transactional Analysis Journal*, Vol. 2 (2).

English, F. (1975) 'The Three Way Contract', *Transactional Analysis Journal*, Vol. 5 (4), pp. 64–7

Frankl, V.(1962) *Man's Search for Meaning*. London: Hodder & Stoughton.

Gibran, K. (1969) *The Prophet*. London: Heinemann.

Goulding, R. & Goulding, M. (1975) 'Injunctions, Decisions And Redecisions', *Transactional Analysis Journal*, Vol. 6 (1), pp. 41–8

Goulding, M. & Goulding, R. (1982) *Changing Lives Through Redecision Therapy*. New York: Grove Press.

Holloway, M.M. & Holloway, W.H. (1973) *The Contract Setting Process* in The Monograph Series of Midwest Institute For Human Understanding Inc. Medina, Ohio: Midwest Institute for Human Understanding

James, M. (1977) 'Treatment Procedure' in *Techniques In Transactional Analysis*. Reading, Massachusetts: Addison-Wesley Publishing Company.

Khaler, T. (1975) 'Drivers: The Key To The Process of Scripts', *Transactional Analysis Journal*, Vol. 5 (3), pp. 280–4.

Karpman, S. (1968) 'Fairy Tales and Script Drama Analysis', *Transactional Analysis Bulletin*, Vol. 7 (26).

Loomis, M. 'Contracting For Change', *Transactional Analysis Journal*, Vol. 12 (1).

Mahler, M., Pine, F. Bergman, A. (1989) *The Psychological Birth Of The Human Infant*. London: Maresfield Library.

McNamara, J. & Lister-Ford, C. (1995) 'Ego States And The Psychology Of Memory', *Transactional Analysis Journal*, Vol. 25 (2), pp. 141–9

McNeel, J. (1976) 'The Parent Interview', *Transactional Analysis Journal*, Vol. 6, pp. 61–8.

Mellor, K. (1980) 'Impasses: A Developmental and Structural Understanding', *Transactional Analysis Journal*, Vol. 10 (3).

Munro, R.L. (1955) *Schools of Psychoanalytic Thought*. New York: The Dryden Press.

Novellino, M. & Moiso, C. (1990) 'The Psychodynamic Approach to Transactional Analysis', *Transactional Analysis Journal*, Vol. 20 (3).

Schiff, J.E. (1975) *Cathexis Reader: Transactional Analysis Treatment of Psychosis*. London, New York, San Francisco: Harper & Row Publishers.

Schiff, J.E. & Schiff, A. (1975) 'Frames Of Reference', *Transactional Analysis Journal*, Vol. 5, pp. 290–94.

Steiner, C. (1974) *Scripts People Live*. New York: Grove Press.

Steiner, C. & Kerr, C. (Eds) (1976) *Beyond Games and Scripts. Eric Berne, Selections from his Major Writings*. New York: Ballantine Books.

Steiner, C. (1979/81) *Healing Alcoholism*. New York: Grove Press.

Steiner, C. (1981) *The Other Side Of Power*. New York: Grove Press.

Stewart, I. (1992) *Eric Berne*. London: Sage Publications.

Stewart, I & Joines, V. (1987) *TA Today*, Nottingham: Lifespace Publishers.

Stuntz, E. (1973) 'Multiple Chair Technique', *Transactional Analysis Journal*, Vol. 3, pp. 105–8 .

Swede, S. (1977) *How To Cure – How Eric Berne Practiced Transactional Analysis*. Corte Mader, California: Boyce Productions.

Tilney, Tony (1998) *Dictionary of Transactional Analysis*. London: Whurr Publishers Ltd.

Woollams, S. & Brown, M. (1978) *Transactional Analysis*. Huron Valley: Institute Press.

Index

Page numbers in *italics* refer to figures, (*n*.) indicates notes.

Skills in Person-Centred Counselling & Psychotherapy

Janet Tolan
Liverpool John Moores University

Skills in Person-Centred Counselling & Psychotherapy is a step-by-step guide to counselling practice using the person-centred approach. The book takes the reader through the counselling process, providing advice on how to structure and manage therapeutic work in ways which are thoroughly grounded in person-centred principles.

The book describes all aspects of the therapeutic relationship – from the initial meeting and assessment, right through to ending the relationship well – and demonstrates how the skills and attitudes of the person-centred practitioner are used effectively in a range of counsellor-client interactions. Psychological contact, congruence, empathy and unconditional positive regard – central tenets of the approach – are defined not only as the basis of counselling but also of the practitioner's wider role within their organization or agency.

January 2003 • 160 pages
Cloth (0-7619-6117-8) • Paper (0-7619-6118-6)

Skills •●●● in Counselling & Psychotherapy

Series Editor: **Francesca Inskipp**

SAGE Publications Ltd, 6 Bonhill Street, London, EC2A 4PU, UK
order post-free **www.sagepub.co.uk**